THE 12 MAGIC SLIDES

SECRETS FOR RAISING GROWTH CAPITAL

Paul M. Getty

Apress·

The 12 Magic Slides: Secrets for Raising Growth Capital

ISBN-13 (pbk): 978-1-4302-6484-2

ISBN-13 (electronic): 978-1-4302-6485-9

Trademarked names, logos, and images may appear in this book. Rather than use a trademark symbol with every occurrence of a trademarked name, logo, or image we use the names, logos, and images only in an editorial fashion and to the benefit of the trademark owner, with no intention of infringement of the trademark.

The use in this publication of trade names, trademarks, service marks, and similar terms, even if they are not identified as such, is not to be taken as an expression of opinion as to whether or not they are subject to proprietary rights.

While the advice and information in this book are believed to be true and accurate at the date of publication, neither the authors nor the editors nor the publisher can accept any legal responsibility for any errors or omissions that may be made. The publisher makes no warranty, express or implied, with respect to the material contained herein.

President and Publisher: Paul Manning
Acquisitions Editor: Jeff Olson
Editorial Board: Steve Anglin, Mark Beckner, Ewan Buckingham, Gary Cornell, Louise Corrigan, James DeWolf, Jonathan Gennick, Jonathan Hassell, Robert Hutchinson, Michelle Lowman, James Markham, Matthew Moodie, Jeff Olson, Jeffrey Pepper, Douglas Pundick, Ben Renow-Clarke, Dominic Shakeshaft, Gwenan Spearing, Matt Wade, Steve Weiss, Tom Welsh
Coordinating Editor: Anamika Panchoo
Copy Editor: Kimberly Burton-Weisman
Compositor: SPi Global
Indexer: SPi Global
Cover Designer: Anna Ishchenko

Distributed to the book trade worldwide by Springer Science+Business Media New York, 233 Spring Street, 6th Floor, New York, NY 10013. Phone 1-800-SPRINGER, fax (201) 348-4505, e-mail orders-ny@springer-sbm.com, or visit www.springeronline.com. Apress Media, LLC is a California LLC and the sole member (owner) is Springer Science + Business Media Finance Inc (SSBM Finance Inc). SSBM Finance Inc is a Delaware corporation.

For information on translations, please e-mail rights@apress.com, or visit www.apress.com.

Apress and friends of ED books may be purchased in bulk for academic, corporate, or promotional use. eBook versions and licenses are also available for most titles. For more information, reference our Special Bulk Sales–eBook Licensing web page at www.apress.com/bulk-sales.

Any source code or other supplementary materials referenced by the author in this text is available to readers at www.apress.com. For detailed information about how to locate your book's source code, go to www.apress.com/source-code/.

Apress Business: The Unbiased Source of Business Information

Apress business books provide essential information and practical advice, each written for practitioners by recognized experts. Busy managers and professionals in all areas of the business world—and at all levels of technical sophistication—look to our books for the actionable ideas and tools they need to solve problems, update and enhance their professional skills, make their work lives easier, and capitalize on opportunity.

Whatever the topic on the business spectrum—entrepreneurship, finance, sales, marketing, management, regulation, information technology, among others—Apress has been praised for providing the objective information and unbiased advice you need to excel in your daily work life. Our authors have no axes to grind; they understand they have one job only—to deliver up-to-date, accurate information simply, concisely, and with deep insight that addresses the real needs of our readers.

It is increasingly hard to find information—whether in the news media, on the Internet, and now all too often in books—that is even-handed and has your best interests at heart. We therefore hope that you enjoy this book, which has been carefully crafted to meet our standards of quality and unbiased coverage.

We are always interested in your feedback or ideas for new titles. Perhaps you'd even like to write a book yourself. Whatever the case, reach out to us at editorial@apress.com and an editor will respond swiftly. Incidentally, at the back of this book, you will find a list of useful related titles. Please visit us at www.apress.com to sign up for newsletters and discounts on future purchases.

The Apress Business Team

I dedicate this book to my wife, Jan, my partner in life and business and my best friend.

Contents

About the Author

Based in Silicon Valley, **Paul Getty** is a managing director at Satwik Ventures, an advisory and investment firm focusing on late-stage companies that are utilizing JOBS Act legislation to raise growth capital. The Satwik Ventures team has invested in 45 firms, resulting in over $1 billion in exits via IPOs and acquisitions. Paul also co-founded First Guardian Group (FGG) in 2003, a real estate investment and management firm focusing on the development, selection, and management of over $800 million of commercial real estate offerings.

His prior operating experience spans over 25 years as a serial entrepreneur and executive officer in firms that resulted in investor returns of over $700 million through multiple successful IPOs and M&As.

Paul holds an MBA from the University of Michigan and a bachelor's degree in chemistry from Wayne State University. He also completed post graduate studies in physics and electrical engineering. He has resided in Silicon Valley for over 30 years and is a well-known speaker, investor, and strategist.

Acknowledgments

I would like to first acknowledge and thank Jeff Olson and Apress for the opportunity to present the ideas and suggestions in this book to a wide audience.

Over my past 30-plus years as an entrepreneur and investor based in Silicon Valley, I have been fortunate to be exposed to many best practices related to raising capital. The 12 Magic Slides approach that is presented in this book is a product derived from attending many hundreds of investor presentations over 20 years—and then working with my colleagues in the venture capital industry to refine the pitch process to best meet the needs of professional investors. There are far too many people to mention who influenced the concepts in this book, but suffice it to say, many of the Valley's top investors and serial entrepreneurs have directly or indirectly contributed to helping me develop the time-tested principles presented here.

I would, however, like to single out three individuals who worked directly with me over the years that these concepts were being developed. The first is Gary Nankin, my fellow co-founder of Venture Navigation, a boutique investment bank formed in the 1990s. Along with our fellow members, we formalized the first versions of the presentation materials as we worked directly with hundreds of young firms and helped them pitch their business ideas to the Valley's VC community.

Over the past twelve years, I have had the pleasure to work with and learn a great deal from one of my current partners, Dinesh Gupta. Dinesh has provided invaluable insights to help refine the basic ideas. He also worked with me to take these concepts to other sectors, including real estate and manufacturing, and also to later-stage firms. We discovered that the ideas in the 12 Magic Slides are equally effective in helping to raise capital in any business sector, regardless of the stage of the business.

I would also like to thank my wife and business partner, Jan Getty, for her encouragement and support over the 10-plus-years process of completing this book. There were many days when she helped to keep our business projects moving forward while I was otherwise distracted working on this book.

I hope that I have not offended anyone for lack of singling them out. I am fortunate to have many respected friends and colleagues who are involved in growing, funding, or otherwise supporting new businesses. I thank all of you who have influenced me in any way to contribute to this book

Introduction

Let's start with a few questions:

- Are you a founder/principal who is seeking to raise external funds for your company?

- Are you prepared to take a fresh look at the value proposition your firm offers to outside investors and, if necessary, rebuild your story from scratch?

- Are you willing to take a hard look at your own presentation skills and take appropriate corrective actions to deliver a more compelling story that stands up to investor scrutiny and wins them over?

There are many sources of advice on how to raise funds for growing companies, both general and specialized, that appear to cover just about every aspect of fundraising that is needed. Most entrepreneurs will start the process of raising funds by first investing time in gathering articles, suggestions, and tips from a variety of sources, and then settle on a format that feels comfortable to them. Then they will assemble a fundraising PowerPoint that they believe covers all the recommended bases.

However well-intentioned these efforts are, the results almost always fall far short in delivering results. Many entrepreneurs are also too proud to solicit external advice or coaching, and/or believe that because they are smart, they can figure out how to best organize and deliver the fundraising presentation.

Beginning with my own direct fundraising efforts shortly after arriving in Silicon Valley many years ago, and then sitting through literally thousands of fundraising presentations as an investor, board member, consultant, and venture capitalist, it became glaringly obvious to me and many other investors that the vast majority of fundraising pitches do not succeed. In spite of the high IQs and fancy academic credentials of the presenters—or maybe because of them—even many very experienced entrepreneurs struggle and fail to capture the right formula for attracting investments in their firms.

Mistakes That Turn Off Investors

The most common mistakes fall into the following categories.

Entrepreneurs seeking funds...

- Fail, in the precious opening minutes, to create a positive first impression.

- Deliver a lengthy "boiling the ocean" story rather than succinctly delivering the key essentials that matter most to investors.

- Present "trapped door" topics that cause investors to lose interest.

- Omit critical investor topics that must be in all initial presentations.

- Fail to seek professional coaching.

- Display poor presentation skills.

Fortunately, all of these areas have proven "best practices" solutions that, once learned, can set you apart from others and significantly enhance your success rate in gaining traction with investors. This book covers them all.

The contents and suggestions in this book are, in fact, largely based on an analysis of successful fundraising pitches that were delivered to groups of sophisticated Silicon Valley investors during the height of the dot-com Internet boom in the late 1990s. At the peak of this period, investors could attend group meetings several nights a week and see as many as ten or more companies present at each event. Sponsors for these events had to limit presentation time to allow all companies to present—and that process forced the development of tighter presentation formats that pitted companies against each other to obtain desired follow-up meetings with funding sources. It was rare that any money was actually raised on the spot; the primary objective of these presentations was to succeed in securing follow-up meetings with qualified investors to more fully present details and due-diligence information.

The challenges of presenting successful pitches were recognized by many of the larger Valley organizations, including the larger law firms, accounting firms, and angel groups that often hosted these fundraising events. Many began offering seminars and "boot camps" to teach their clients how to optimize their stories so that they could be more effective in raising their funds, which were, in part, used to pay fees to these service providers. At the time, I was CEO of Venture Navigation, a boutique investment banking firm that assisted firms with obtaining growth funds. After establishing a good a track record of success in helping firms raise capital, we were approached by the accounting firm Deloitte Touche to establish an "accelerator" program to develop a curriculum of classes for entrepreneurs. This quickly became an effective finishing school on how to not only raise money, but how to hire great employees, motivate teams, understand financials, be a great CEO/CFO, and so forth. The most popular and best attended workshops were those in which we presented the fundraising ideas presented in this book.

We saw many rapid transformations in the hundreds of firms that we worked with, and it became clear to us that much of the secret sauce of fundraising could be effectively learned—even by the nerdiest entrepreneur. As an added and somewhat unexpected benefit, the process of developing a more effective fundraising pitch often led companies to modify—or in some extreme cases even abandon—their business strategies altogether and seek more successful directions. It also became apparent that developing a good pitch can be a very stressful process and amplify discord between core team members. That's because during the process of building a winning pitch, objective and often harsh realities need to be confronted not only at a business level but also at a personal level, and many entrepreneurs in our classes were simply not up to the required tasks. Better to know this early in a firm's existence rather than in the midst of a crisis.

From this start, and from the hundreds of presentations I've seen in the dozen-plus years since the dot-com bust, come the principles outlined in the book. In short, they work—and not just for technology start-ups, but for all types of firms at any financing stage up to and including raising funds for public firms.

Essential Elements

While the techniques of developing and presenting a successful fundraising presentation can be learned, in order to achieve success, you must also have a strong story to tell. Key elements include:

- A capable and credible leadership team that possesses sufficient prior experience to convince investors that it can overcome challenges and deliver results. The team includes not only the chief executives, but also committed advisors, board members, and well-known supporters of the firm that provide needed validation.

- A clearly defined and large, growing market for the firm's products and services.

- Differentiated key factors for successful market penetration possessed by the firm that have been validated by significant industry segment participants.

- Realistic financial goals along with recent history of meeting and/or exceeding prior expectations.

A great presentation cannot overcome deficiencies in any of these key areas. If need be, therefore, put off your fundraising efforts until your story becomes much more attractive to investors.

Is This a Good Time to Raise Funds for My Company?

The answer to this most common of questions is an unequivocal "Yes and no."

Seriously, the answer is "Yes" if the firm and its team are ready, even over-prepared, to earn the commitment of outside investors. In my experience of watching market cycles over more than a 30-year period, general market conditions, no matter whether good or bad, do not correlate well with effective fundraising. Regardless of the times, there always appears to be more money than good deals. As a result, good companies with good stories and good teams seem to be able to get the job done. Indeed, some of the best companies were started in relatively tough times:

- Apple
- Founded in April 1976
- US unemployment rate: 7.7%
- Prime rate: 6.8%
- Oracle
- Founded in June 1977
- US unemployment rate: 7.2%
- Prime rate: 6.8%
- Intuit
- Founded in May 1983
- US unemployment rate: 10.1%
- Prime rate: 10.5%
- Cisco

- Founded in December 1984

- US unemployment rate: 7.3%

- Prime rate: 11.1%

At the time of this writing, late 2013, the stock market is making all-time highs, the IPO pipeline is robust, and there are a growing number of investors and investment groups flush with newly minted cash that they want to put to work. Although unemployment and chronic deficits remain very high, the US is experiencing a resurgence of optimism and the creation of new companies and related funding opportunities in places like Silicon Valley is approaching levels not seen since the dot-com boom of the late 1990s.

However, the process of raising funds remains very challenging due to the large number of firms seeking investment, and many investors still have scars from the 2008 crash. A track record is much more important than it used to be. During the dot-com bubble, if you were right out of Stanford with no track record, you could get between $2 million and $5 million for a good dot-com start-up idea. Today, you better have strong customer validation and team members that have done it before.

Note It's always a good time to raise money—if you have strong fundamentals and have prepared well for meetings with investors. But while there is capital to be raised, be aware that investors, scarred by the events of 2008 and later, are risk averse. Even if you have a great idea and a strong team, expect to work hard to secure the money you need to grow.

Ironically, given the overall challenges of fundraising in the current climate, many entrepreneurs have far too casual an attitude toward fundraising and think that if they have good idea, investors should be chasing them. Big mistake! Many companies still don't invest in professional fundraising services, opting instead to rely on casual introductions to investors and key investor groups from a few people on their board, or from friends, or from their attorneys or accountants. While some of these people may be able to arrange a first meeting, they typically don't have the time to get involved in helping the process or fill the gaps as the process evolves. As a result, many first meetings are also the last meeting.

Another critical insight that is often missed by firms seeking funding is that investors usually only review and fund deals referred by their network, and they favor those referral sources who have a history of bringing high-quality deals with a lot of the due diligence already done. Firms attempting to get to first base by mass mailings of business plans are almost 100% guaranteed to fail in securing sought-after investments. Therefore, most firms are well advised to focus most of their initial energy on locating and cultivating referral sources close to their target investors before directly investing time in sending out plans.

Tip Forget mass mailing business plans. Put time into finding and cultivating people who can refer you to professional investors.

It's a Different World Now

In the go-go days of the dot-com era, raising capital could be done within a few days and with a single-page summary, or sometimes even less. Before approaching investors today, firms need to be thoroughly prepared with almost a full due-diligence package and potentially a private placement memorandum (PPM) that can take even later-stage firms hundreds of man-hours to prepare. In today's climate, firms should expect to invest over a thousand man-hours to secure financing—as well as several thousands of dollars for needed legal assistance. Although money is plentiful, investors are risk averse and more often looking for reasons to say "no" rather than to write a check.

In our work with hundreds of firms over the past several years, we have seen that the biggest mistake a CEO can make in this environment is to try to raise funds using only internal resources, such as his own time and effort. From our perspective, it is virtually impossible for the management team—the CEO in particular—to meet the day-to-day demands of growing a successful firm and also have the capacity to raise large amounts of growth capital in this current market. Something is bound to fail in the process—and often the consequences of under-resourcing the fundraising process leads to companies that hit the wall, and/or CEOs who are asked to step aside.

Many CEOs will seek out assistance from experienced fundraisers to help them with tuning the presentation materials, making investor introductions, and reviewing term sheets, among other items. Often there is a temptation to the let the outside fundraiser run the process and tightly control content and follow-up efforts. In general, this is a mistake because heavy outside management of the process will quickly be picked up by savvy investors and they will conclude that they are dealing with a weak or disinterested CEO.

If you choose to work with an outside fundraiser (and there are many good ones, as well as not-so-good ones), it is even more critical that you study everything in this book, and ask questions and challenge inputs if you are given guidance that takes you off course from the basic principles that are outlined.

> ## ENTREPRENEURS BEWARE!
>
> There are many out-of-work or semiretired executives that moonlight as fundraisers. They are often compensated in stock options for offering assistance. There is a strong tendency to take more control than appropriate since they want to justify larger compensation. These fundraisers will often come to the investor presentations (a red flag for investors) and then weigh in during the presentation to endorse the CEO/company. This is a big mistake, and it often leads to a bad outcome. These presentation meetings are not the place to have a big brother standing in. Investors are not investing in the intermediary—and they know that comments by intermediaries will be biased due to the compensation they are receiving. Their presence wastes time and creates a very poor first impression.

Any firm that is within 12 months of needing new investment capital should already be aggressively planning its fundraising strategy. We see many tragic situations where otherwise great ideas and entrepreneurs run out of runway just a few months short of attaining a critical milestone because they either started the fundraising process too late, or they relied on the belief that insiders and close friends could deliver funds in time.

In spite of the challenges, right now, indeed, may be the best time to start a new company or raise expansion funds for existing companies. The passage of the JOBs Act in 2012 and its many regulatory exemptions for smaller companies, coupled with the growing crowdsourcing movement—which is already having a positive impact to expose companies to more potential investors through firms like Kickstarter, CircleUp, HealthFundr, and so forth—suggest that new fundraising paradigms are about to blossom. I will comment further on several of these new approaches in the chapters ahead.

How This Will Work for You

If you are planning to raise external funds (equity or debt) for a new or existing business at any stage, the insights in this book will be invaluable to you. Its core is a description of the 12 Magic Slides—the slides that describe the essential elements of your pitch and that, combined with your presentation skills, hugely increase the chances that you'll find the capital you need. While the 12 Magic Slides were originally developed to assist start-up entrepreneurs to raise their first rounds of external capital, we discovered that the process worked equally well for later-stage firms and even public company companies that were seeking secondary financing.

During the past ten years, our firm's investors have generally shifted their investment preferences toward later-stage firms, where the time to exit (i.e., realize a return) are less than with start-ups. Many of our investors have also asked us to evaluate making investments in smaller public companies, so-called "micro-caps."[1] As a result, we have been exposed to presentations from many later-stage private, as well as smaller public companies.

Without fail, I have seen even later-stage firms and public firms fail to meet their funding objectives if they stray away from the basic principles presented in this book.

No matter the size of the firm, it vitally important that all 12 areas be succinctly covered in meetings with investors—and that the suggestions for pre-meeting preparation, as well as post-meeting follow-up, are closely followed.

To be sure, more mature companies have more to offer in terms of prior history and product performance, and they can offer additional market validation and more customer feedback than earlier-stage firms. However, we repeatedly see presentations from later-stage firms that do not address the basic 12 areas and most commonly overaddress some areas with too much data, while omitting critical points that, in sum, leave investors unwilling to commit funds.

THE 12 MAGIC SLIDES

Slide 1: Overview

Slide 2: The Problem

Slide 3: The Solution

Slide 4: Opportunity and Market

Slide 5: Technology

Slide 6: Unique Competitive Advantages

Slide 7: Competitive Landscape

Slide 8: Go to Market Strategy

Slide 9: Financial Roadmap

Slide 10: The Team

Slide 11: Current Status

Slide 12: Summary

---

[1] "Micro cap" is short for *micro-capitalization*. Micro cap companies have a market capitalization (shares outstanding × the price of a share) of $50 million to $500 million. These stocks are generally publicly traded over-the-counter (OTC) or on NASDAQ.

We advise later-stage companies to build their presentations by starting with the 12 Magic Slides—and then include additional supporting materials subject to meeting-time constraints, or in follow-up interactions with investors.

We have also seen that the 12 Magic Slides process also works equally well for any type of business—not just technology companies.

Why?

All savvy professional investors have the same basic questions about why they should invest in a new business idea. Indeed, even many friends and family investors will be more willing to invest if you follow the guidelines suggested in this book. Whether you are seeking external funds for a home-based services business or a high-flying technology firm, you must cover the basic 12 areas to have the best chance of getting a check.

How This Book Is Organized

I encourage readers to first take the time to skim through the book to get a general overview of the layout and flow. A more comprehensive reading should follow, after the scope of the process has been grasped. Each section is critical to developing a successful pitch, and there are often subtle dos and don'ts that should be understood and followed. So don't skip anything and make sure you make an effort to complete the recommended exercises throughout the book. Readers are also encouraged to search the Internet at the conclusion of each chapter, using key words in the chapter to find additional relevant information. Once you have finished reading the entire book, you should also begin looking more critically at other fundraising presentations that you see/hear. This is often a good interim step to take before you dive deep into your own presentation, since it is often difficult to see the forest for the trees when looking at one's own presentation materials.

Let's get started!

What Investors Want

There are many types of investors and, at the risk of oversimplifying a complex topic, let me start with two categories: smart investors and dumb investors. That latter category includes, for example, friends and family. Dumb investors are not necessarily bad investors, since they have money and often very good intentions. They tend to invest based on fairly superficial criteria, however, including first impressions, their prior relationships to the CEO and key executives, and they tend to invest funds quickly, often without performing any significant due diligence.

On the positive side, these types of investors can be easier to convince to write a check and, if you have enough of them, you might be able to raise most if not all of your initial capital requirements. Indeed, this is the most common way of getting started and also helps to demonstrate to follow-on investors that you have "skin in the game."

On the negative side, less sophisticated investors can make your life miserable by being overbearing and wasting much of your time with their questions and suggestions. Accepting too many small checks means that you will have that many more phone calls and e-mails to answer. In a worse case, if things go bad, less sophisticated investors can be more inclined to take legal actions to recover losses and you may end up losing close relationships over business matters. A bigger concern is that investors in your next round will want to see a list of all current shareholders and may pass on your deal if they conclude that you have too many unsophisticated investors on board.

This is not a black and white issue, but something that you must be keenly aware of as you raise capital.

The Investors You'll Meet

Smart investors can be individuals investing from their own funds or professionals representing the interests of clients who have placed funds with them. They invest those funds based on a deeper analysis of risks/rewards of each specific opportunity. At the extreme end of this spectrum are highly skilled teams from reputed venture capital and private equity firms with substantial staff resources who will conduct deep and exhaustive research on all aspects of a potential investment before committing funds. Indeed, the commitment of one of these highly regarded professional firms is the highest form of validation that an entrepreneur can receive; an investment from a top venture capital firm can usher in a wave of co-investors and blue-chip service providers who can provide the most likely path to future success.

The first step in developing your fundraising strategy is to realistically match your firm's financial requirements and story to the types of investors that can get the job done. If your goals are modest—for example, starting a work-from-home services business—friends and family investors may be sufficient. However, if you plan to grow a highly successful firm employing large numbers of employees and eventually seek an exit via an initial public offering (IPO), or a merger or acquisition with a larger company, then you need to prepare to deal with highly sophisticated investors. That means building a strong story that motivates them to invest in your firm vs. the many others they evaluate.

As mentioned, the approach to fundraising outlined in the following chapters can apply to small and large firms, as well as already established firms that are seeking further rounds of external capital. However, from this point forward, we will assume that the reader is seeking to attract professional smart money investors. I tailor the suggestions accordingly. A well-constructed story for smart investors should also work very well for "friends and family" types—and will create a better first impression by showing off your ability to develop and present a tight story.

In a nutshell, here is what we have consistently found that attracts the interest of savvy investors:

- CEOs/teams with a good track record
- Strong customer validation (i.e., they are buying the product or service in good numbers)
- A potentially big market for your firm's products or services
- A defensible business model that leads to profits
- A good story, well told

- A big return on investment
- Well-defined exit plans with credible options, as well as projected timing that fits investor expectations

You must prove you have a potential home run to get their attention—and be prepared to score 90% across all of these topics in a pitch that can be delivered in no more than 20 minutes. It's a tall order, but I'll show you how to do it successfully.

Think of the fundraising process as a series of challenges that need to be overcome, step by step, before receiving a check. The journey begins with first impressions followed by investor scrutiny in each of the preceding areas, in approximately the same order of consideration. If you strike out at any level, you will not succeed.

Let's explore each of these areas in more detail.

Is Your Track Record Good Enough?

While the track record of the team and the firm's advisors are very important, savvy investors first focus on the CEO. If he or she can pass muster, then other items will be considered. If not, game over.

In general, here is what investors look for in a CEO:

- Has "been there and done that"
- Has specific domain experience/expertise
- Is aware of knowledge gaps and locates resources to fill them
- Can attract, hire, and manage superstars
- Shows "fire in the belly"
- Desire to succeed and willing to make a 24/7 commitment
- Recognizes urgency in generating revenue minimizing the burn rate (the speed with which a recently funded company uses money)
- Understands the difference between being an employee and being a shareholder
- Brutally honest, with a tendency to under commit and over deliver

Is a college degree required? Investors are well aware of the fact that many successful CEOs lack college degrees. Some of more famous recent examples include:

- Mark Zuckerberg, CEO, Facebook
- Steve Jobs, former CEO, Apple Computer
- Richard Branson, CEO and founder, Virgin Group
- John Paul DeJoria, CEO, John Paul Mitchell Systems
- Michael Dell, CEO, Dell Computer
- Bill Gates, former CEO, Microsoft
- Larry Ellison, CEO, Oracle

However, due to the very high risks associated with most private equity investments, investors will rarely invest in firms led by a CEO without a college degree, unless the CEO possesses other extraordinary attributes in terms of industry experience, previous outstanding accomplishments, or, as in the case of Mark Zuckerberg, a concept so compelling so as to offset his personal risk profile.

Note　You can succeed as an entrepreneur without a college degree, but the hurdles are much higher when it comes to raising money. It's better for most people to put in four years at the best school you can get into. And hey, you just might learn something.

The CEO who possesses a college degree (and ideally an advanced degree from a top school), will be far more likely to advance to the next stages of investor scrutiny. Tightly coupled with an appropriate college credential, personality traits play a critical role in gaining investor interest. Once credentials are established, investors look for CEOs who

- Are charismatic communicators, great deal makers, and are able to attract top talent to work for them.
- Have a high personal energy level with a driving desire to hit targets and inspire over-the-top performance from others.
- Show outstanding personal sales abilities and can close big deals and convey the firm's mission in a compelling manner.

- Understand their personal shortcomings and can surround themselves with talented staff members to form a well-rounded winning team.

- Have a history of attaining important distinctions and racking up personal successes.

John Chambers, CEO of Cisco, is a great example of an extroverted, driving leader who was able to close big deals, and who has a vision and persona that attracts and motivates top talent. Beginning CEOs would do well to invest time studying the traits of great CEOs and picking appropriate role models. When you get stuck and cannot seem to find a solution, it might be useful to ask yourself "What would [your favorite CEO] do in this situation?"[1]

In short, appropriate degrees from notable schools and the right personality will buy you enough time for investors to then consider your experience.

If you are raising money for a firm in an established business segment with notable competitors, experience in your field is critical in winning over investors. Without adequate prior experience, ideally as a former executive in a firm related to your market/technology focus, investors will not believe that you know enough about the inner workings of your business or have a strong enough personal network to be successful.

Many notable executives, such as Jack Welch of GE, Eric Schmidt of Google, Andrea Jung of Avon, and others, became CEOs only after working their way up the ladder in their industry to first establish a strong track record of accomplishments.

If you are raising money for a relatively new business area, your prior life history and ability to show that you can attract top talent will take center stage.

Born in 1984 and becoming a multibillionaire before the age of 30, Mark Zuckerberg is an extraordinary example of a CEO who lacked industry experience—there were not many similar social media firms at the time he started Facebook—yet he was able to convince Accel Partners, a highly regarded venture capital firm, to invest $12.7 million before his concept was even fully developed.

---

[1] Better yet, seek out and establish relationships with successful CEOs. It has been said that CEOs are often the loneliest people in the company since they have no peers that they can confide in—and everyone expects them to always have the right answer to any problem. Check out the Young Presidents Organization (www.ypo.org) and other similar networking groups in your area.

By the time of this investment, Mark had already attained a number of notable life accomplishments that undoubtedly contributed to Accel's interest in investing. These included:

- Creating an Atari-based messaging program called Zucknet at age 12 that was used to communicate with patients in his father's dental office.

- Taking graduate computer programming classes while still in his teens.

- Becoming captain of the fencing team at an exclusive pre-paratory academy in New Hampshire.

- Creating a music program similar to Pandora while in high school. Firms, including AOL and Microsoft, expressed interest in purchasing it—along with offering him employment as a teenager (which he declined).

- Developing Course Match while at Harvard, which allowed students to pick classes online, and Facemash, which allowed users to vote on which one of two faces was most attractive.

While an undergraduate at Harvard, Mark had already demonstrated an ability to attract highly talented people to work with him, including Dustin Moskovitz, Chris Hughes, and Eduardo Saverin, who became the co-founders of Facebook.

He is also the only entrepreneur that I know that had a major motion picture depicting his early career completed before he turned 30!

Rather than be depressed by comparisons to Mark Zuckerberg, I hope that those of you who have the right stuff are energized and motivated by this background summary! As stated, this is an extraordinary example that led to the creation of billions of dollars of wealth at a very early age.

You certainly don't need all of these attributes and life successes to become a fundable CEO.

The important takeaway is that you must begin your CEO aspirations with an honest personal audit of what you have accomplished and what you plan to accomplish in order to earn the trust of investors. And it is never too early or too late to start that process.

The Bottom Line

Although some individuals are born leaders, investors will most likely invest in firms whose CEOs have a prior track of doing much of what they are expected to do in the future. It is critically important for you to take stock of yourself as a CEO against the criteria listed earlier so that you can shore up areas that can otherwise be obstacles that will doom your hopes to raise capital. While you may the next Steve Jobs or Mark Zuckerberg and get funded in spite of shortcomings in these highlighted areas, the odds do not favor it.

If you come up short, all hope is not lost if you have a truly compelling business proposition. It might be better, for example, to first recruit a stronger CEO candidate for your firm and focus your personal core competencies where you truly excel, such as engineering, sales, or finance. Getting your firm funded, followed by providing an acceptable return to investors, should ultimately be your top priority. Those who recognize this early will be far more successful in their careers.

Strong Customer Validation

The success of any company is ultimately determined by its ability to attract customers for its products/services. Your funding presentation must therefore include information on target market segments and why customers in those identified markets will be attracted to your value proposition. The less theoretical and speculative you can be, the better.

Most investors are attracted to firms that plan to become dominant leaders in their defined markets and are less inclined to invest in "me-too" firms. If you are aspiring to grow a large publicly traded company, or one that may be acquired by a large company, your target market segments must be large enough to allow you to grow to $100 million–plus with modest market penetration. Most presentations that capture the interest of top VCs, for example, identify billion-dollar-plus market segments and detail plans to capture 5% to 15% market share within five years. That equates to revenue run rates in the range of $100 million.

Another way of looking at this is to realize that professional investors who invest high growth in early-stage firms are generally looking to realize a ten times return on their invested capital. If the investment is being made at later stage, like the last round before a pending IPO, the required returns may drop to three times due to less time required to realize a return of capital plus profit.

Obviously these metrics can only be achieved if you can demonstrate that you have substantial proof of the likelihood that large numbers of customers will buy your products.

Obtaining strong customer validation and demonstrating that you have "traction" in the marketplace is therefore a critical early step in developing your fundraising pitch. As you approach this task, invest time with your team to first validate who your best target really is. Often, the first "customers" are low-hanging fruit, but they may not be the best highest potential customers that you should use to develop your business plan.

As an example, we have recently worked with a medical device company that has developed a new method for detecting vascular disease. Their first customer focus was on general physicians. As their marketing efforts evolved, they received feedback from some of their physician customers, who told them, "Your marketing is all wrong. You are missing the biggest segment." The company then learned that physicians who derive income from government-backed health-care plans like Medicare receive much higher compensation after detecting vascular disease than physicians who offer more traditional fees for services and who seek reimbursement from insurance companies. This insight led the CEO to refocus his firm's marketing strategy on a much larger—although narrower—segment, which increased excitement from investors and paved the way for an early IPO to raise expansion capital. That would not have been possible with the original customer focus.

This story underscores something important: the CEO should frequently revisit the focus of the firm on its target customers and help guide his team to hit the best bull's-eye possible. During the life cycle of many companies, the target market is evolving and they must make many ongoing corrections to keep their strategy in line with changing customer needs.

When investors ask you about "traction," they are really asking you to provide hard evidence of actual customer interest. Short of having a current revenue stream and related references, the next best way to demonstrate traction is to present quotes and references from potential customers and industry insiders on the merits of your offerings and why they will do business with you. Without such external validation, you will not be able to demonstrate traction nor capture much investor interest. And that, in the eyes of investors, validates your solution and shows them you do, in fact, have a business.

■ **Tip** Constantly monitor your target customers. Their needs are changing on a daily basis, which means your offerings or approach may need to change as well. If you lose focus, you'll find your business on the rocks.

Sources of Validation

The hierarchy of validation that investors seek is generally in this order:

- Customers
- Partners
- Channel intermediaries
- Industry consultants
- Other credible insiders

Not all of these of course are equal. Weak customer validation, for example, cannot be easily overcome, even if all remaining groups are positive. And validation that directly supports your company's underlying value proposition is more valuable than corroboration that indirectly suggests customers might ultimately adopt your solution. As shown in Figure 1-1, the most impactful form of validation is when you can demonstrate that credible nonrelated customers have objectively evaluated your offerings and have decided to pay your price for obtaining the benefits of products/services.

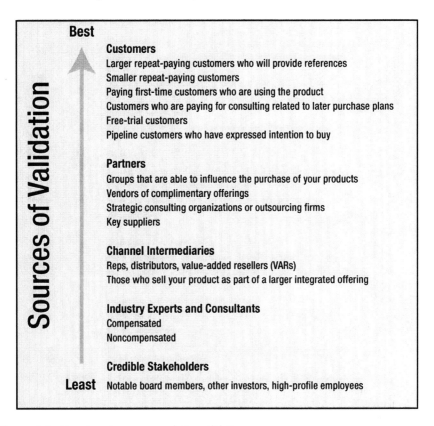

Figure 1-1. How investors assess relative validation sources

If you are unable to provide customer validation, you then need to focus on partners, followed by channel intermediaries, and so on, and build your case as strongly as you can in the order shown.

I want to stress, however, that it is virtually impossible to be funded unless you can include at least some level of customer validation along with added support from these other sources of validation. If you are stuck, flex your creativity to create opportunities for customers to provide meaningful feedback on your solution.

As an example, many potential customers should have interest in at least trying your product for free before committing to buy it. Many Internet- and software-based offerings plan for extended periods of free trails by customers before the start of actual revenues. If you decide on this approach, make sure you do a good job of collecting feedback to reinforce your value proposition and your planned pricing model. Free trials also have a downside in that they can impact the perceived value of your products and possibly attract larger competitors earlier than desired. However, the risks can be easily managed. This free trial/survey approach is a very common way of proving to investors that you have created something that is actually desired by potential paying customers.

If your product is more complex and you need funding to build a prototype, there are still many ways to obtain meaningful customer feedback, even if you need to resort to drawings, pictures, videos, and so forth. Fortunately, with the plethora of software modeling programs and applications like Photoshop, it is possible to create very lifelike depictions of just about anything that can be imagined.

A winning presentation should primarily focus on customer validation, but touch on all other areas. We will go deeper into this important area in Chapter 2.

Identifying a Big Market for Your Firm's Products and/or Services

Presuming you have adequate customer validation, investors will want to know the number of additional similar customers you may be able to develop. Put another way: How big is your market?

This discussion should include an analysis of the Total Available Market (TAM) and Served Available Market (SAM) for your products/services. As an example, the TAM for an online bookstore might be all those that who purchase books (obviously a huge market). However, the SAM might be only English-reading book buyers in the United States between the ages of 12 and 70 who have incomes above $20,000 per year. Once a SAM is identified, it is common to discount the size even further by limiting the projected market penetration (also called Share of Market or SOM) to relatively small percentages, like 5% to 10%. Generally, larger estimates invite more scrutiny and skepticism, so it is best to see if you can build a compelling plan that is based on large well-defined markets with only modest penetration.

The size of your defined market must closely correlate to your stated business model and projected return on investment (discussed shortly). For higher-risk technology firms, investors often want to see a SAM of $1 billion or more with penetration projections supporting company revenue of $100 million within five years. For less risky business ventures, or ones where returns may include an ongoing income stream (e.g., dividends), investors will be satisfied with lower returns. In all cases, investors will also look at the internal rate of return (IRR) on their invested capital (further discussed later in this chapter).

Before gathering data on the size of your target market, it is helpful to first work backward to determine how large a market you need to provide required returns to investors, as well as provide sufficient growth capital for your firm to reach its objectives. A simple version of this exercise would consist of the following steps:[2]

- Create a simple spreadsheet of expected revenues, costs, and net profits over a five-year period.

- Determine how much external capital is required to fund your company until you get to break even.

- Presume the value of your company will be four times gross sales in the fifth year.

- If needed, adjust revenues to that investors can achieve a ten times return on their invested capital in five years.

- Multiply the fifth year's income ten times to determine a rough market size that will be needed to allow investors to achieve their target returns (assuming 10% market penetration).

Figure 1-2 will help you prepare your projections.

---

[2]This example presumes a higher risk technology firm. If your business is less risky, investor expectations can be reduced.

Five-Year Projections
[Date]

Income Statement	2013	2014	2015	2016	2017
Net sales					
Cost of goods sold					
Net operating income					
Operating expenses					
Net income					

Cash Flow Statement	2013	2014	2015	2016	2017
Beginning balance					
Cash inflow					
Cash outflow					
Ending cash balance					

Balance Sheet	2013	2014	2015	2016	2017
Cash					
Accounts receivable					
Inventory					
Prepaid expenses					
Total current assets					
Fixed assets					
Total assets					
Accounts payable					
Short-term notes					
Accrued and other liabilities					
Total current liabilities					
Long-term debt					
Other long-term liabilties					
Total long-term liabilities					
Shareholders' equity					
Total liabilities and equity					

Figure 1-2. A basic form for creating financial projections five years out

This is a *very* rough cut of what you may need to identify a target market— and only a starting place that you will need to refine as you develop a deeper understanding of your business model. However, this short exercise can be a real eye-opener and provide you with a critical reality check as to whether you have a business that will attract investment capital—or not. An important related exercise is to assemble data on similar companies that have successfully obtained investments, and then see how your projections compare.

Tip Stop now and do the exercises required to estimate the size of your market, your potential penetration into it, and your potential financial results five years out. If your revenue at that point isn't sufficient to meet investor requirements (i.e., $100M+ if you are a riskier technology firm), you're probably not going to raise capital from smart money investors in today's fundraising climate.

Armed with this data, you should then take an objective look at the market for your products and services, and prepare to build a strong case that there is sufficient demand to meet investor objectives. In addition to direct research that you perform, many entrepreneurs are well advised to commission a third-party market study that can evaluate market trends and competition, and determine what slice of the pie you may be able to grab. If your market already has competitors and other similar investments, it is likely that market studies have already been completed, which may be helpful for you to build your case to investors.

Be sure to talk to analysts and business writers in your segment to gain insights and save time. Investors will require third-party validation of your projections, so it is important that you begin to establish relationships with credible business analysts outside of your firm as early as possible.

Defensible Business Model

One of the first filters that investors apply when looking at a company is whether the offering is a feature, product, or business. Features don't make a product and can be copied easily. Similarly, investors understand that a product doesn't make a business. Attractive businesses have a slew of products, and a road map for how to create customers. Attractive businesses also have appropriate infrastructure—planned or already in place—including talented developers, salespeople, customer support, designers, and finance, operations, and logistics professionals.

The combination of the firm's talent pool, the nature of its revenue model, and steps taken to protect its intellectual property is what converts it from something that can be easily copied into something that can start to be defensible. Be prepared to have a strong answer to the question, "What stops others from following and dominating the market you discovered?" Many attractive markets are full of established companies that have substantial resources and the ability to access and serve your firm's target customers.

So, how do you stop a large company that wants to move into your space? Often you cannot. You are left with two scenarios. Either you have a structural advantage from being the first mover. Or you simply have the best execution, which can involve a decent amount of luck at the right time. eBay is a great example where first-mover advantage in a new market nearly eliminated the opportunity for others to catch up.

To establish that you have a defensible business, you need to have good answers to the following questions:

- What is your unique intellectual property and how do you protect it? Do you have patents?

- Can your service be easily reproduced by a competitor?

- What defensible advantages do you really have? Algorithms? Data? Customer experience? Security?

- What is the strength of your employee talent pool and key advisors?

- What is your underlying asset? What happens if it becomes commoditized?

A Good Story, Well Told

Investors see hundreds of presentations by talented entrepreneurs and also have much firsthand experience working with successful CEOs and management teams. As such, they quickly develop a keen sense of what makes a good CEO. A good CEO will not guarantee funding, but a bad CEO will almost certainly kill any chance of landing needed investors. Whether consciously or not, investors will strive to quickly develop a first impression about the CEO that is usually binary. In other words, if the CEO performs well in his presentation, the firm will gain further consideration and, if the CEO does not perform well, game over.

Early in my investment career, it was more common to encounter technically brilliant CEOs who did not present especially well—but who were still able to close on funding due to their engineering skills. Today the standards are much higher and a CEO needs to not only have a good story, but an ability to communicate it well and establish that he/she has those magic CEO attributes similar to other successful CEOs known to the investor.

As I will discuss in a later chapter, an excellent way to begin a funding presentation is for the CEO to tell a brief story about the company that immediately conveys that an attractive investment opportunity is about to unfold. Investors will quickly evaluate the story-making skills of the CEO since they understand that they are watching a performance that will be used in various flavors not only to attract investment, but also to convey the vision and purpose of the company to attract and effectively manage the highly talented employees who will be needed to make the firm successful.

While your persona as CEO will become clearer to the investor over time, during your initial meeting you need to strive for a great first impression. Here are my top ten suggestions that will get you off to a good start in a first meeting with investors:

1. **Do your homework.** Start by thoroughly researching the profile of the investor well before you begin your presentation. Use the Internet, personal references, service providers, classmates, and so forth. It is human nature to be attracted and warm up to people that start introductions with acknowledging that they know something about you. Better still if you have common friends or acquaintances that you can offer up in your opening seconds. Example: "John Richardson, my advisor at Santa Clara University, indicated that he worked with you on a recent project. He said to say 'hi' and that he would be available to talk with you about his interest in our solution."

    If you are presenting to a group, open with relevant comments about the group (positive references from others, prior successful investments), and know who the key decision makers are and acknowledge them. Strive to make sure investors mentally check off the "did your homework" box in your opening minutes. That makes a great first impression.

2. **Arrive a few minutes early.** Showing up late, especially to a first meeting, can create a bad vibe that is difficult to overcome. Traffic or not, investors equate punctuality with good organizational skills. If you are really stuck in an unexpected delay, use your cell phone to call ahead. When you arrive early, engage the receptionist to loosen up if possible and take time to "get in your zone."

3. **Dress appropriately.** The safest advice in this area is to make an effort to dress in a similar manner to what your investor is likely to be wearing. Even if you are meeting with West Coast investors, where dress codes are very relaxed, you can negatively impact your first impression by either underdressing or overdressing relative to your audience. Your first investor presentations will undoubtedly be preceded by many similar presentations that you have personally observed—so there should not be much mystery on how other entrepreneurs typically dress in similar settings.

4. **Emphasize good "body English."** Ever watch a movie with the sound turned off and notice that you can still understand a good deal of what is going on? That's because the majority of what people communicate is done so by their body gestures and overall image. Your body English must be in sync with your verbal communications and give off an overall impression of confidence and credibility. Some tips:

   a. **Posture:** Look relaxed, but stand tall and maintain good eye contact while smiling. Focus on your investor more than on your presentation materials.

   b. **Handshake:** Deliver a firm handshake while making eye contact.

   c. **Body gestures:** Move your hands and arms appropriately as you talk. Watch videos of your performance and also seek professional coaching to improve your overall presentation techniques.

   d. **Miscellaneous:** Other things investors look for are poise, any indication you are uncomfortable, eye contact, body language that fits your words, and so forth.

Early in my career, I had the benefit of professional coaching on how to deliver great presentations. One of the most important areas was watching videos of my performances while my coach would make suggestions on how to improve my overall body language. I learned that—just as all fingerprints are unique— each person has a distinct body language profile. However, that profile can and should be professionally optimized and you should seek out professional coaching, if possible. At a very minimum, take videos of your presentations and request candid and objective feedback from more experienced presenters whom you admire.

There is nothing embarrassing in asking for assistance in this very important area. However, it can be tragic to watch an otherwise well-prepared and experienced new CEO go down in flames through using poor or inappropriate body language during an important investor presentation.

5. **Use your voice properly.** Speak deliberately but not too quickly, and balance your passion with a controlled confident tone to your voice. Practice key pitch points by recording your voice and make appropriate adjustments to modulate your voice to emphasize important items.

6. **Cut the small talk.** Get down to explaining how you can make money for the investor. Don't chitchat about the weather or other nonrelated topics.

7. **Know your pitch inside and out.** Practice until you deliver all needed points without notes. Have good answers to likely questions/objections prepared in advance.

8. **Make sure your presentation materials and overall "look and feel" are top-notch.** Invest in having a qualified specialist produce a final polished version of your slide deck and any leave-behind materials. Similarly, do not get started with fundraising without first updating and polishing your firm's web site with professional assistance. Investors will look at your web site before they look at you. Some will want to see your slide deck in advance or have other materials provided to them before you arrive. All of these need to be first class.

9. **Encourage interaction.** Don't make the mistake of presenting a monologue. Get feedback as you move forward through your presentation while you have the attention of the investor. Don't wait for it to come afterward. Expect to receive negative comments and be prepared to overcome objections with solid answers, if possible. Investors are usually looking for reasons to not invest or to find holes in your story to weaken valuation expectations.

10. **Follow up.** The biggest mistake you can make is to avoid following up after your meeting. Indeed, look for opportunities to deliver items or facts asked by your investor. At the close of your meeting, provide a brief summary of other items that you will provide and also when you will provide them. Avoid getting too aggressive on setting commitments. It is better to be more general ("by later this week" than "by 10 a.m. tomorrow morning"). Savvy investors will test your ability to honor such commitments—so take them very seriously.

A Big Return on Investment

Harvard senior lecturer Shikhar Ghosh did a study in 2012 of about 2,000 companies that received venture funding between 2004 and 2010 and found that about 75% of start-ups fail to return invested capital, let alone provide any profit to investors.[3] Given these high failure rates, investors and others who fund start-ups must invest in only those firms they believe will provide very high returns to offset losses on the remaining investments that will not be successful.

What, then, are acceptable returns?

Riskier technology start-ups need to generate a minimum ten times return on invested capital in no longer than ten years to be considered suitable investments. In fact, ten years is the outside limit for returns that would be tolerated, since many professional funds only fund their management fees for ten years. A ten times return in five years is the more common criteria that is used when looking at presentations, since investors need to assume that there will be delays and that initial projections are always rosier than reality. That means you'll need to show such excellent returns in five years in your pro formas, even though investors will be giving you some slack and may be willing as long as ten years to get the hoped-for returns.

If the investment is in a later stage, say the last private round before the company breaks even, or goes public, or is sold, the minimum return can drop to two to three times, depending on the specific situation. Also if your business opportunity is lower risk (e.g., a group of experienced bankers who are opening a new regional bank), the expected returns can be adjusted accordingly.

An investment of equity will generally require higher returns than an investment of debt. This is because a debt investment—for example, a loan that the firm chooses to take from a lender—is usually conditioned on having a higher priority of return than the return of equity. If the company is liquidated, first funds typically go out to pay debt holders and remaining funds go to equity holders. Many debt investments also require ongoing payment of interest, whereas equity investments typically are paid upon a future exit.

How Investors Compare Investments: Internal Rate of Return (IRR)

An excellent tool for comparing needed returns at different stages of the life cycle of a company is to look the internal rate of return, or IRR, on the invested capital.

---

[3]http://online.wsj.com/news/articles/SB10000872396390443720204578004980476429190

The most basic and common way in which professional investors compare potential investment options is to first perform IRR calculations. Everything else being equal, the investment with the highest IRR value is considered to be the most preferred one to make.

IRR is derived by looking at the total cash flows of the project over time, starting with the cash that is initially invested and the subsequent cash flows that occur over time until there is a final return of all invested cash and profit.

From a mathematical standpoint, IRR is the discount rate at which the Net Present Value (NPV) of the cash that is invested equals the Net Present Value of all the cash inflows that will be derived from the investment.

Once the IRR is calculated, it is used as follows:

- If the IRR is greater than the cost of capital, that is, the minimum rate of return required by the investor, the project is economically sound.

- IRRs of various investments are compared and those with the highest values will be generally preferred over those with lower IRR values.

While IRR is a very important consideration, it is only one of the factors that are considered along with other more subjective data points.

While an explanation of IRR and other advanced finance topics is beyond the scope of this book, what follows is a quick, basic primer.

In order to calculate IRR, you need to first determine the net cash flows (C_n) that will be realized over a defined future period (n). Common periods are usually a year, a quarter, or a month. It is helpful to develop a table that starts with first showing invested cash as a negative value, followed by all the subsequent cash flows for future periods from the investment as positive values (see Table 1-1).

Table 1-1. Cash Flow over Three Years

Year (n)	Cash Flow (Cn)
0	-1,000,000
1	3,00,000
2	5,00,000
3	5,00,000

The variables of period and cash flow (n, C_n) are then placed into this equation, where N is the total number of periods and IRR is calculated by determining the IRR value that yields a Net Present Value (NPV) of zero.

$$NPV = \sum_{n=0}^{N} \frac{C_n}{(1 + IRR)^n} = 0$$

As an example, let's presume that that we are investing $1,000,000, and then receiving back positive cash flow at the end of each of the three years.

Then the IRR or r is given by:

$$NPV = -1000000 + \frac{300000}{(1 + IRR)^1} + \frac{500000}{(1 + IRR)^2} + \frac{500000}{(1 + IRR)^3} = 0$$

In this case, IRR = 0.1319, or 13.19%.

The mathematically astute reader may quickly realize that this formula is best solved using successive approximation of the IRR value (i.e., substituting different IRR values until the calculation yields a value of 0).

A much faster approach is to use the IRR function in Microsoft Excel, once cash flows along with related time periods have been defined. There are many references on the Web about how to calculate IRR using Excel, and also on YouTube if you wish to learn more.

While each investor group can be expected to have its own IRR requirements, IRRs in the high teens to low twenties are typically in the range of what most professional investment firms expect to generate for their investors for higher-risk investments, such as in young companies. Higher objectives may be set, however, for screening new investment opportunities.

Note   Most investors will be looking for an IRR in the range of maybe 17–23%. Do the math yourself before you face investors, so you'll have the confidence to ask them for the money you need.

How Investors Compare Investments: Multiple of Cash on Cash

An alternate "quick and dirty" means of comparing investments is to look at cash-on-cash returns—the ratio of total annual cash flow to the initial investment. Investors will be seeking a certain multiple of cash returned based on cash invested. While professional fund managers evaluate their performance on IRR, it is also common to hear investors taking about a ten times or "10X" return. These types of comparisons, of course, omit the time value of money that is highly relevant to comparing investments; however, this "cash on cash" comparison remains very common in casual conversations.

See Chapter 4 for a more in-depth discussion of investor returns.

Well-Defined Exit Plans

Investors expect firms they invest in to build something significant and to take it to exit. Exit, in this sense, means realizing the increased value in the invested equity of the company in a liquid form, like cash or other cash equivalents (public stock that can be freely sold). It is this future value—along with the time to achieve liquidity—that attracts investors. From the earlier summary of IRR, you should now understand that a large return many years out may be less attractive than a smaller return in a shorter period of time.

While the eventual exit of your firm may occur in ways that you cannot accurately foresee, investors will nevertheless expect that you present plausible exit scenarios along with a timeline that will allow them to calculate an IRR to compare your deal with others. Your exit plans need to be clear at the founding of the company, because they will dictate how you operate it. For example, if you plan to become a publicly listed company, you should follow generally accepted accounting practices from the beginning in order to avoid costly and lengthy reformatting of historical documents.

Possible exit options include the following:

> **Go public through an initial public offering (IPO).** With the passage of the JOBs Act in April 2012, a number of the former constraints to going public were removed. As a result, many firms that had not previously considered an exit via an IPO have now made this objective their preferred exit plan. A full discussion of the use of the new JOBS Act legislation is beyond the scope of this book. However, readers are strongly encouraged to evaluate JOBs Act–related IPO options as they prepare their exit strategies. Traditional IPOs can cost anywhere from several hundred thousand to several million dollars, plus require ongoing annual costs ranging up to hundreds of thousands of dollars per year. The JOBs Act promises to reduce these costs significantly and increase the dwindling number of US IPOs.

Merger or acquisition (M&A). The expectation in an M&A transaction is that 1 + 1 will equal more than 2. In other words, the combination of two firms will generate greater value to investors than the standalone firms by themselves. In recent years, many more companies have provided returns to their investors through an M&A transaction than by going public. Therefore, it often makes sense to focus at least some of your strategy on identifying and cultivating potential acquirers of your business. While it is true that companies receive offers from larger accompanies without any proactive effort on their part, investors will expect you to have a good story in this area, so be prepared. As we will discuss later in the book, an M&A with a firm that places a high value on what your firm brings to it can create one of the fastest paths to extraordinary returns for you and your investors.

In order to understand how acquisition can produce a greater exit value than an IPO, let's look at the concept of accretive value. *Accretive value* is the value of an acquisition based on the added value that is provided to the acquiring company. This is a very important concept that can catapult the potential value of your company to a specific acquirer. It can best be understood by considering the following example.

In the spring of 2013, Yahoo! announced the acquisition of Tumblr for $1.1 billion. The microblogging platform produced $13 million in revenue in 2012. It may seem ridiculous to pay such a high amount for a company with such paltry revenues, but Yahoo! justified the value by betting that its acquisition of Tumblr will attract a younger audience and the ad dollars that come with them. As Ken Goldman, Yahoo!'s chief financial officer, said at a conference shortly after the acquisition was announced, "Yahoo! needs to be cool again. Gaining Tumblr's young audience will help Yahoo!'s brand, and it will allow the company to sell data on a coveted demographic to advertisers."

This is a powerful example of how a relatively young firm with limited revenues can realize a very high exit value. The value of Tumblr through a future IPO is unknown—but its value to Yahoo! was clearly very high due to added revenues that they would be able to derive due to synergy with other products and services. Furthermore, they were able to obtain an exit without having to wait for an IPO, which may have not have occurred for some time longer, if at all. Sometimes companies acquire other firms because they can, and sometimes they do so because they need to. This acquisition seems to fall into the latter category—Yahoo!'s "portal" model of directing users to news stories from the site's home page is declining as more people get their news through social media and the acquisition of

Tumblr may have been needed to allow Yahoo to accelerate changes in their business model to built greater stockholder value.

Your first presentation to investors (or even your more detailed offering materials) do not need to project values on potential accretive values to potential acquirers. However, if you conclude that an acquisition is the most likely exit path for your firm, you should be prepared to comment on this strategy in general terms and provide the names of potential acquirers along with listing some reasons why those firms could realize value from an acquisition.

Summary

You need to begin the process of building your presentation by first gaining a thorough understanding of what your target investors want to see in both your business proposal and what they expect to see in you as the CEO. Realize that most investors are seeking to find holes in either your business concept or in you or your team. In other words, they are looking for reasons to say "no." Writing a check is an exception that comes only after all the possible reasons to say "no" have been exhausted.

Other tips include:

- Don't be too quick to take checks from less sophisticated investors. Consider that every check obligates you to that investor going forward.

- Before you start pitching, make an honest appraisal of your shortcomings and your ability to successfully convince investors that you can lead your company. You may be better off being a successful second fiddle than a failed conductor.

- Plan to make a significant investment in honing your presentation style. Once developed, good presentation techniques will last for the remainder of your career and beyond.

- Develop an understanding of the hierarchy of business validators that investors look for, and focus your early marketing efforts on targeting strong referenceable and paying customers. Paying customers are your most important trump card in convincing investors.

- Make sure your attainable market share fits the objectives of your target investors in advance of first meetings.

- Be prepared to explain how and when investors will receive both a return *of* their investment as well as a return *on* their investment!

Building External Validation

In Chapter 1, I discussed the importance of including a discussion of customer validation in your investor presentations. To convince investors to back you, you need credible third-party confirmation that your solution is not just good but viable in the marketplace. In this chapter, I would like to go into greater detail on how this is best accomplished. To recap, I presented the following hierarchy of validation sources:

- Customers
- Partners
- Channel intermediaries
- Industry experts and consultants
- Other credible stakeholders

Let's discuss each in more detail.

Customers

Whether you think you have the most appealing technology or not, you are going to have to prove that the dogs will eat the dog food. Validation falls into a number of areas, but the number-one source must be users or potential users of your solution. Your best source of validation is satisfied, paying customers from your highest-value target segment.

Got customers already? Good, but be aware that a firm's first customers are rarely the best customers, which are defined as those who are willing to pay the highest value for the firm's products/services. More frequently, early customers are not good validators since they may 1) not have paid full price; 2) have had less than satisfactory experiences with an early release; 3) be smaller customers than what the firm needs to target; 4) be in a market subsegment that does not represent the highest and best use.

Doing business with any of these types of customers is not necessarily a bad decision in the early stages of the firm's life cycle. Indeed, it may make sense to initially work with smaller, less-desirable customers with the anticipation they will be guinea pigs and likely to discover problems in the offering that need to be addressed before more strategic customers are approached.

Before you approach investors, it is critical that you build a list of target customers and segment them to meet the needs of both the company and investors. A simple A-B-C ranking system can be used. "A" customers represent those that will be most valuable to land, and "C" customers are the desired early adopters but not your long-term target. This exercise is by no means limited to start-ups, since every fundraising round you'll ever have needs to cover customer validation. Even if a firm is well along in its life cycle with established customers and revenues, it should still go through periodic rankings of its customers. You need to focus on capturing a larger number of those customers that will provide the highest net value, as well as dropping customers who are costing you more than they are worth.

The investor presentation should focus predominantly on discussing your A-list customers. Testimonials and references should be drawn exclusively from this group, if possible.

■ **Tip**   When meeting investors, present customer validation—sales figures, testimonials, and so forth—from your A-list customers. These are the people and companies that will buy your solution at full price and make the most of it.

Partners

For purposes of this discussion, *partners* are the commercial entities who are not direct buyers or channel intermediaries of your products/services, but groups with which your firm has a close relationship or alliance. Partners influence your business strategy. Your relationship with them may be contractual, or it may be a loose arrangement designed to project a larger image to potential customers.

Business partners can be

- Key suppliers.

- Vendors that sell related, complementary products.

- System integrators.

- Strategic consulting organizations or outsourcing firms (e.g., a call center).

- Marketing alliance partners that are part of an industry coalition to establish needed standards and best practices.

If the group of business partners adds notable credibility to the firm's funding story, include their names/logos in the funding presentation. If some may become important strategic customers or acquirers of the firm in the future, it may make sense to comment on them briefly. More often, however, business partners are less important to cite than key customers. So, in some cases, you may not mention them at all in the funding presentation. But you should still feature them on your web site and in the due diligence materials you will present after gaining initial investor interest.

Channel Intermediaries

Examples of channel intermediaries include resellers, manufacturers' representatives, distributors, value-added resellers (VARs), and industry-specific vendors (ISVs).

It is important to call these out in your presentation if they have the potential to significantly and positively impact your financial results. For example, maybe they will become an acquirer, or perhaps they will bring desirable customers that may significantly add to the firm's value upon exit.

Some words of caution about channel intermediaries, however: intermediaries should generally not be your first salespeople. Look upon them more as strategic customers and do not approach them too early. Early products often have bugs or performance gaps, and it is important for the firm's direct personnel to deal with these issues and not work at arm's length through intermediaries. If you stumble with an intermediary, it can be difficult to recover and may create negative industry stigma that can impact value and impede market penetration.

Tip Remember that sales are your responsibility first. Don't "outsource" sales to channel intermediaries, who may not have your passion or your best interests at heart. It's also important that you are in a position to solve customer problems directly and not at arm's length through an intermediary.

As the firm grows, monitoring the cost of selling will become more important and the balance between using direct vs. indirect sales channels needs to be carefully managed. The growing use of the Internet has generally created a bias toward going direct, and many intermediaries are being squeezed out of their roles. Even Tesla is now challenging the longstanding indirect dealership sales distribution model in automobile sales and is attempting to go direct, even in states where such practices are currently outlawed. Therefore, anticipate and be prepared to answer questions from investors about your sales strategy and use of intermediaries vs. direct channels.

Industry Experts and Consultants

Investors will expect that you are closely connected with credible industry experts and will contact them during their due-diligence process prior to making investments. Negative remarks for prominent experts or, worse, comments like, "What is the name of the company again? I'm not sure I know about them," can mean the end of the road for your funding plans.

The process of developing relationships with credible experts should have started earlier in your career. As a CEO, you are, after all, presumed to have significant industry experience and be well known to sector analysts. However, it is also true that many experts come and go over time, and you must periodically refresh old contacts and meet new ones.

Tip Start cultivating industry experts now. They can not only provide essential insights and referrals as you grow, but these relationships will serve you well when fundraising. Industry experts are in positions to corroborate your assertions and projections, as well as confirm that you are a worthy leader.

The best way to establish and maintain good relationships with industry experts while you are busy running a growing company is to selectively attend and present at conferences. Speaking at conferences and participating on panels often requires you to help sponsor the event. However, it's money well spent. If you are a speaker, you and your firm will gain much more visibility and you likely meet more key people than as just an attendee.

One of the biggest challenges facing small companies who elect to exit via IPO is obtaining analyst and media coverage for their firms to support desirable stock prices and trading volumes. Experts who cover and report on smaller public companies typically fall into a unique class all by themselves. Many sectors have anointed rock-star stock analysts and market makers who you must get to know and who can be very influential in assisting your firm to meet its value creation objectives.

Even if you do not plan to exit via an IPO, seek these people out and make sure they at least know what your firm does. Stay in periodic touch with them. They make a career of being industry insiders and will occasionally be aware of important new trends or moves by larger companies who are seeking to acquire smaller firms. They can also be a good source of referrals if you need assistance accessing another high-level industry executives.

Prior to the move toward the decimalization of stock prices in the mid-1990s, there were many more analysts who covered smaller issuers and whose firms received related compensation from the larger bid/ask spread on their shares. The ranks of these analysts have rapidly dwindled in the ensuing years as decimalization effectively dried up compensation. The few analysts that remain often earn their fees by being directly engaged by public stock issuers to report on their companies. Concerns over conflicts of interest in these types of relationships abound and there has been a recent movement, as part of the JOBs Act of 2012, to allow smaller firms to increase their bid/ask spreads (also call "tick size"). Once this occurs, expect many new analysts to enter this field, and look for opportunities to establish new relationships with them because they may become valuable resources for you/your firm.[1] If you choose to go public at some point, having several of these analyst relationships in place will prove to very helpful.

Other Credible Stakeholders

This category includes board members and key advisors as well as important value-add investors such as larger firms who have made an investment in your firm.[2] They can (and should) be supportive, but don't forget that they may also have the power to kick you out of your CEO role or push for other changes

---

[1] I strongly encourage you to research the writings of David Weild and his colleagues on the issues that have been created by decimalization, as well as his insightful suggestions on how to fix this serious issue. A good introductory article is found in the SEC archives at www.sec.gov/info/smallbus/acsec/acsec-backgroundmaterials-090712-weild-article.pdf.

[2] One of the largest sources of value-add investor investment is IntelVentures, an investment arm of the Intel Corporation (NASDAQ: INTC), one of the largest semiconductor firms in the world. They tend to invest in companies that can provide strategic advantages to them, for example, a new graphic chip that they can integrate into a new microprocessor. They not only invest, but can provide very significant assistance as the firm grows.

that you may not support. So, to the extent you can, pick them wisely and stay close to them with frequent interactions, including sharing both good news and bad. The most frequent source of friction between stakeholders and management is a perceived lack of communication and transparency—and the buck stops at the CEO's desk.

I recommend that all CEOs participate in a CEO networking group.[3] One of your objectives in participating is to be aware of how other CEOs optimize their communications with all stakeholders—especially those who can influence strategic decisions. Best practices in this important area are ever-changing, but the core fundamentals remain the same: setting and then reporting on business expectations in a credible and predictable "no surprises" manner. Consider this a critical part of your outreach to board members and investors.

Testimonials

Once you decided on whom to consider as a validator, you need to decide the form their validation will take. You can

- Cite them as available for a phone call or meeting.
- Offer a reference letter or a quote by them.
- List the name of the firm as being a key customer.

Before discussing the structure of a good reference, let me point out that the problems that most firms solve for their customers fall into one of the following categories.

If you are primary selling to other businesses (B2B), your products/services will do one or more of the following:

- Increase revenues
- Lower costs
- Improve market penetration
- Offer a not-for-profit societal benefit that may be desired by some groups

If your customers are primarily consumers or direct individual users (B2C), your products and services will typically be purchased because they

---

[3]One of the best known networking organizations for CEOs is the Young Presidents' Organization. Check them out at http://www.ypo.org/ and consider joining them.

- Provide a perceived tangible consumer benefit (faster, cheaper, more fun).

- Enable the buyer to perform a desired activity (golf clubs, tools, musical instrument).

- Satisfy an emotional desire (prestige, cool factor, etc.).

In the hierarchy of testimonials that can be given, B2B firms that can reinforce that your products and services increase their revenues will be viewed by investors more favorably than the other areas listed. That does not mean that you will not get funded if your offerings do not increase revenues but instead, say, lower costs. It is just something that you need think about in evaluating those customers that you wish to put forward as the best validators.

Another consideration is the degree to which a customer agrees that they have a significant problem that is solved by using your products. Ideally, identify customers that can make these three key assertions:

1. **The Problem: "Yes, Company X is addressing a significant problem in our industry…"**

   By acknowledging a large problem in their industry segment (not just a "one-off" that may work only for them), they validate that your company's focus is a good one.

2. **The Budget: "We've committed Y dollars to fix this problem (or gain this advantage) …"**

   Through indicating that they have already committed dollars to invest in a solution that you propose or already offer, emphasizes urgency and at least some degree of prior research to determine what they are willing to invest.

3. **The Solution: "We've hired [your company] to fix the problem…," or, second choice, "We are prepared to hire [your company] to fix this problem upon meeting certain specifications."**

   It's a powerful statement to indicate that they have already researched various options and selected your firm among other firms as their preferred solution provider. What's more, they have committed dollars or are prepared to commit dollars subject to some minor improvements or tests (which you are likely to easily achieve) to invest in your solution. That emphasizes urgency and at least some degree of prior research to determine what they are willing to invest.

After reviewing your A-list customers against these added considerations, you will be better armed to determine which customers to cite to investors.

B2C firms that can demonstrate a model that provides large-scale adoption and acceptance along with the generation of profits will be most attractive. As an example, one of the main reasons for the attractiveness of Facebook to its early investors was the rapid growth trajectory of their first subscribers. Revenues were not as important initially since the investors saw that the potential for rapid acceptance would quickly lead to lucrative advertising revenues. Initial validation from advertisers, including iTunes and Google, helped generate strong investor interest.[4]

For those that you judge to be best for direct phone calls or meetings with investors, coaching is absolutely vital, because what these customers say can and will control your destiny. Do not make the mistake of simply turning over customer contacts and letting investors go at them without first providing guidance to the key contact. Until the investment funds are in your firm's bank account, continue to operate with a healthy degree of paranoia and assume that investors are looking for reasons to say "No." Presume that the wrong comment from a key customer can end the due-diligence process.

■ **Tip** Until you have money in the bank, operate with a degree of paranoia; assume that what can go wrong will, and take steps to mitigate the possibility. This goes double when it comes to handing out your customer references' contact information to potential investors. A bad call can result in an investor walking away, so prep your reference as best you can.

Once you have determined which customers to use as references, you and your team should write out a script of what you would like them to say, keeping the preceding points in mind. Your script should also include a list of anticipated questions and answers. For example, your Q&A might cover the following:

- The severity of the problem

- The value of a solution (and your solution in particular)

- Budgetary issues (cycle, dollars available) that affect purchase timing

- The decision-making process for buying the solution

---

[4]Facebook then went on to win over many application developers as advertisers, who were able to encourage Facebook users to download their new applications within Facebook. This led to a large boost in income from mobile devices, which helped propel Facebook's stock well above its IPO price.

- Market assessments

- How your product/service compares to other solutions

- Any concerns the customer may have in dealing with early-stage companies

- Other items unique to your situation

Once this has been finalized, call or meet with your contact to go over the points that you wish them to emphasize verbally, as well as to get their feedback. Sense their comfort level on each point before concluding your interaction with them. After the meeting concludes, send an e-mail highlighting the points in writing that you have discussed with them. Some investors are very slow in contacting customer references, and days or even weeks might go by before your investor contacts your referral customers. Having the points in writing will help ensure good recall of the key points that you wish them to emphasize. Be sure to follow up with your customers to obtain their feedback on the call with investors, as well, and obtain details on what was of interest to the investor and how your customer felt about the call.

Summary

The single most important area that investors scrutinize is the external validation that you provide to them, including references from key customers, partners, channel intermediaries, and credible stakeholders. By now you should understand the following:

- How investors weigh the different types of references and other validating data that you provide.

- How you should go about obtaining the best possible sources of validation.

- Proven ways to ensure that your references will reinforce the key points that you wish them to make.

Having a good understanding of the information in these first two chapters will allow you to make critical decisions on whom to target as ideal investors for your firm. Even if you are not the next Facebook, all the tips and suggestions provided thus far will prove helpful in getting you closer to realizing your desired funding objectives.

Identifying the Right Investors

In late 2013, the time during which this book is being written, we are witnessing a renaissance of creative fundraising methods and options for firms of all sizes. With the passage of the 2012 JOBs Act, the Internet has been abuzz with literally hundreds of new ways of connecting entrepreneurs and investors, especially for early-stage investing. Predating the JOBs Act, firms such as Kickstarter, with their innovative prepayment funding approach, have ushered in and legitimized the process of using crowdfunding techniques to raise investment capital.

The past ten years have also seen an explosion of hedge funds and private equity firms that focus on later-stage investing. Firms such WR Hambrecht have also dusted off and updated the Dutch Auction process and applied it to raising funds for well-known firms, including Google and Pete's Coffee. Sentiment in Congress and within the SEC appears to favor permitting even more flexibility and creativity ahead to help reestablish capital formation and much-needed jobs growth in the United States.

The growth and spread of social networking with sites such as LinkedIn and Facebook provide expanded opportunities to network and get connected with investment groups as well. It has never been easier, in fact, to locate and connect with target investors. As a result, entrepreneurs have a rapidly growing number of funding options available to them.

The Landscape of Investment Firms

At the highest level, professional investment groups segment themselves based on the stage of the financing cycle where they wish to focus. Figure 3-1 is a good diagram that summarizes the full range of where investors focus.

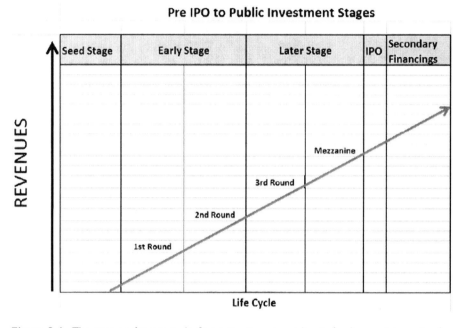

Figure 3-1. The start-up finance cycle. Some investors specialize in funding certain parts of the cycle

Generally, investment firms will narrow their focus to specific market segments the later in the financial cycle that they choose to invest. The number of investment firms is also greater for earlier-stage investments than for later stage, since returns can be better for those firms that succeed.

The types of equity investment groups fall into the following categories:[1]

- **Angel investors.** Angel investors are typically wealthy, successful former entrepreneurs who seek high returns through making seed-stage and early-stage investments. Many angel investors prefer to invest jointly with other

---

[1]Adapted from SBA.gov, Caron Beesley, "Five Tips for Finding and Securing Private Investors for Your Start-Up," http://www.sba.gov/community/blogs/community-blogs/small-business-cents/five-tips-finding-and-securing-private-investor.

angels, often with other members of various angel organizations that exist in larger cities across the United States. Angels have characteristics in common with professional gamblers in that they are willing to sustain significant losses in order to achieve occasional, ultra-high 10X or more returns.

- **Venture capital (VC).** Venture capitalists also tend to focus on making seed-stage and early-stage investments. But unlike angel investors who invest their own funds, VCs primarily invest funds that they have raised from large institutional investors, such as state pension funds, universities, large private companies, and so forth. VCs are able to invest more time and attention to each of their investments since they receive a management fee of 1% to 2% of their invested funds and can therefore hire research staff and other personnel to perform deep due diligence prior to making investments. Unlike angels, VCs typically take board seats and are often deeply involved in reviewing and guiding company operations. See Chapter 4 for a more complete discussion of venture capital.

- **Private equity (PE).** PE is often confused with venture capital. In contrast to VC investing, PE firms (e.g., hedge funds, merger and acquisition (M&A) firms, real estate investment trusts [REITs], etc.) typically invest in later-stage and, often, public firms that they can reposition for a profit through downsizing, merger with a larger firm, changes of key executives, and so forth. These groups are more risk averse than VCs and rarely participate in early-stage investments.

- **Government programs.** There are a wide variety of funding programs available from federal, state, and local governments. These range from outright grants of capital with no requirement to repay, to programs that provide low-cost loans. Although TV commercials and web sites promote "no strings" capital from government-related resources, such claims will prove false under closer examination. For the most part, funds obtained under these programs must be invested in activities that lead to a perceived positive and approved social outcome. Also, almost all such programs require ongoing reporting and compliance activities, which, if not met, can result in the recall of some or all of the capital, and possibly even fines or other penalties.

The best known and most widely used government capital sources for small business is available through the Small Business Administration (SBA). These programs are best suited to "bread and butter" businesses, as opposed to high-risk technology start-ups, where risk levels are off-set by a strong likelihood of a return of invested equity or debt. Read more about SBA programs on its web site at www.sba.gov/content/sbic-program-0. The Small Business Investment Program may be of particular interest to entrepreneurs.

- **Debt financing.** As discussed elsewhere in this book, all entrepreneurs should consider and utilize debt financing as appropriate to their specific situation. While obtaining needed funding by borrowing money can be less costly than raising capital by selling ownership interests (e.g., equity), there are important tradeoffs related to the increased liability of the borrower(s) to repay the loans. For many entrepreneurs, especially those located in regions that are not near sources of angel or venture capital, borrowing capital via credit card debt or a home equity line can be viable options.

How to Find Potential Investors

Although it has never been easier to find potential investors, hard work is still required to find the right ones. Your objective should be to reach investors through common referral sources and warm introductions, rather than cold calling or "confetti marketing" methods.

You must build a database to capture and organize contact data, as well as capture notes and summaries of your outreach efforts and interactions. I personally prefer building a simple Microsoft Excel spreadsheet, which is then updated at least daily. If you are more comfortable with a formal client relationship management (CRM) system, and have significant prior hands-on experience with a specific package, feel free to use it.

▩ **Caution** I have seen too many fundraisers get bogged down with learning a new software package and unnecessarily delay the start of the process. A down-and-dirty "ready, fire, aim" approach works best. Figure 3-2 shows a typical format that I have successfully used to raise hundreds of millions of dollars.

Target Investor List					Active		
Possible Lead Investor?	FIRM	CONTACT	TITLE	PHONE	EMAIL	Exec Summary Sent?	Status/Next Steps
X	ABC Ventures	Diane Veesee	Partner	650 222-23XX	dveesee@abcventures.com	X	In process -- PG meeting with them next week
	Angel Investor Club	Joe Angel	Individual	650 752-55XX	jangel@aol.com	X	PG to FU this week
	Loan Link	Steven Lenderoff	VP	650-321-86XX	steven@llink.com		Left voicemail
X	Seasoned Capital	David Mark	GP	650 234-99XX	david@seasonedcaptial.com	X	First meeting here next Fri

Figure 3-2. Fundraising contact information spreadsheet

Start by mining all of your team's business contacts who may have direct connections with investors, including service providers (attorneys and accountants, for example), other executives, clients, vendors, industry connections, former colleagues, friends, and family.

Once this is complete, it is time to tap into the Internet.

Here's what I think works best.

CrunchBase and AngelList

Go to CrunchBase (www.crunchbase.com) and AngelList (www.angel.co) and get very familiar with all that they offer. In my opinion, CrunchBase is the more powerful of the two sources. It provides details about potential investors and the types of investments they are actively making. Enter the names that you just gathered and see what comes up. Here's what you're looking for:

- Where they are located (many investors only invest within two hours of their location)

- How much money the firm has to invest and where it comes from

- Personal bios

- Contact information

- An investor's personal investments

- Prior employment history

- Types of investments that they have led

- Names of firms that they have invested in

Track down CEOs of companies that have received funds from the investor and contact these CEOs to understand their experiences and suggestions. Most CEOs that have received funding are more than glad to share insights with you. Be sure to first send an introductory e-mail letting them know who you are and why you are interested in talking with them. If you can, approach them through either a warm introduction from a common contact—or at least reference a common contact in your introductory e-mail.

Make an effort also to contact entrepreneurs that have been turned down by the investor. It is good to understand the deals that investors don't do, as well as the ones that were successful.

Tip   Look carefully at the deals investors make. It will tell you a lot about what they are interested in—and the kinds of deals they shun.

Limitations of Internet Searches

Although you may find the names of desirable investors via the Internet, don't expect to find the required contact information. Many high-profile investors are hard to locate via conventional Internet searches on Google, Linked-In, Facebook, and so forth. Also, data from social networking sites on "friends" and people you apparently mutually know can be very unreliable. Well-known investors are often inundated with business plans and executive summaries, and unless a funding proposal comes through a warm contact, they will likely not look at it. Instead, use the Internet to find more about their backgrounds and hunt down ways to connect with them via a common contact—or perhaps by referencing a common interest such as a hobby, community activity, charity, church, and so forth.

One of your best sources of warm introductions can be well-known service providers, such as law firms, accounting firms, investment bankers, and traditional banks who work with smaller firms (e.g., Silicon Valley Bank). These types of organizations are generally relatively easy to approach ("Hi, I am Joe Entrepreneur and I would like to explore establishing a business relationship with your firm. We seek client managers who are well connected with local investors. Who do you recommend?") The larger and better-known firms sponsor and/or host networking events (to be discussed shortly) and their better-known lead partners are often asked to speak at conferences where they meet and establish relationships with investors.

These groups are hungry to establish new relationships and are an excellent source of contacts and related background information on target investors.

Tip   Add the names of target investors to a daily Google search. Over time, you will discover more information about them (e.g., an announcement that they will be speaking a local event, or news about a new company that they have funded, etc.), which may improve your ability to contact them.

Networking and Meet-up Events

Unless you live on a secluded mountaintop in the middle of nowhere, you probably have access to various networking events near you, where investors, service providers, and entrepreneurs mingle. In smaller cities, locations near college campuses are common for these meetings. In larger cities, law firms, accounting firms, industry associations, and media firms often host these events, often with no charge for admission and sometimes even with drinks and snacks. These days, such events are easy to find by Googling key words. People based in Silicon Valley are fortunate to have many such events hosted in the greater Bay Area each week, and the opportunities to meet fellow investors and entrepreneurs are endless. Exchanging business cards or snapping pictures of contact information on smartphones for follow-up later is a terrific way to further develop your network in a relatively low-cost and often fun manner.

Conferences

Whereas conferences can be expensive to attend, and many investors who participate may not be suitable (for example, they do not reside in your geographical area), your fundraising budget must certainly include some of these events. I rarely attend conferences unless I have a speaking slot. Sometimes I have a booth as a way to be more visible than regular attendees and to set myself apart from others. This allows for better opportunities to be memorable and to also meet the key people. Next to new, solid investor contacts that you might make, the most valuable take away at a conference is the list of attendees, along with their contact information (e-mail and phone). Better yet, get the list of registered attendees in advance, study it, and highlight all the key people that you need to meet while there. An attendee list with contact information is most coveted, and it is typically only given to sponsors and speakers. But there are many ways for resourceful people to obtain these lists, which I will leave to your own creativity to figure out.

As passionately as you are seeking investors, realize that investors are also actively looking for new deals and can be expected to participate in conferences and seminars as well as in local networking events—especially where they may be speaking.

Tip   Never forget that investors are looking for new deals. In most cases, they want to know more about you and your company. So don't be afraid to approach a potential investor—but be ready to have the conversation that could change your life.

Regardless of the source of the investor contact, I want to reemphasize the importance of obtaining a referral from a credible source to raise receptivity to your story. Using your spreadsheet, periodically group all potential investors from outside your network for whom you do not have a warm referral sources. Send it around to all those within your network to see if you can find a common connection. Become a member of LinkedIn and identify any common connection that exists between you or management team members, and potential investors as well. However, verify that a common contact indeed knows the person you are trying to connect with. It can be embarrassing to refer to a common contact from LinkedIn who is not known to the other party. Cold calls and e-mails should only be used to fill dead time. But recognize that usually they just create a false sense of progress. If your story does not click with warm referrals, you will have little hope of success with cold calls.

Determining Investor Suitability

Before you invest too much time chasing investors, be sure that the types of investors you are seeking have a profile of making investments in firms such as yours. As an example, if you're seeking to raise less than $1 million for your business, spend time focusing on friends and family, angels, smaller investment firms, lenders, or crowdfunding.

Many entrepreneurs are far too casual about selecting their investors. Yet the selection of the right investors may be one of the most important decisions that a company makes and the process needs to be elevated to the highest level of scrutiny. Why?

- Professional investors will be among your most important personal references going forward in your career. Whether your company succeeds or not, your key investors will be there to provide references on you for new ventures. Assume that all key investors will be contacted by all those who invest in your future investment rounds, as well as any new companies that you get involved in as a key executive.

- Good investors have a knack for turning lemons into lemonade. Even if you run out of resources to get your firm to an exit, a good investor can often find a company that will buy what you have developed.

- If you impress investors with your skills and abilities, they can plug you into new opportunities that can increase your string of hits. If they form bad impressions of you, consider your career as a CEO to be terminally damaged.

- Unless you are one of the really rare entrepreneurs who have hit after hit, or who has one megahit that seals your future, presume that your investors will remain influential in your future career—for better or worse.

In order to determine whether there is a good fit, the following are several questions every entrepreneur should take into consideration when actively raising funds from professional investors.

Does the Investor Click with You and Your Team on a Personal Level?

Like other close relationships, the personalities of your investors need to mesh. There needs to be a deep level of understanding and chemistry, otherwise it will never work. Be careful about making snap judgments on first impressions. Just as investors will size you up over multiple interactions and perform thorough background research on you/your team, you must do the same with them. A good way to accelerate this process is to ask questions such as, "What do you like about my company?" "Can I talk to three or four CEOs you recently funded?" "What causes you to consider replacing a CEO?" "How often and in what manner do you prefer to communicate with executives about your investments?"

Even if you are seeking money from investment clubs or angel groups, be sure to get the names of companies they have recently invested in and make it a point to seek out and talk with the executives of those firms. And ask for the names of the last four companies that members have invested in, and go talk to those entrepreneurs.

What Can/Will They Bring to the Table?

Make sure you not only totally understand what an investor can bring to the table, but also what they are willing to specifically commit to your deal. It is not sufficient just to examine their track record in working with their investments, since patterns of involvement are often deal-specific and change over time. One very hands-on investor that I knew made a big killing and was off to Italy shortly thereafter to build a large, fancy chateau. Needless to say, his availability to his other entrepreneurs was compromised in the process and much of what he could have done to help was not possible.

Too much involvement, even from well-intentioned investors, is also something to be cautious about. Famed entrepreneur Richard Branson of Virgin cautions entrepreneurs to be wary of overly meddlesome investors. His advice: "Bear in mind that a dictatorial financial partner can dim the spirit and enthusiasm of a new enterprise, muffling the spark that prompted you to launch this project—the spark that is most likely to make your venture different from your competitors."[2]

Vinod Khosla, one of the most well-known and successful venture capitalists in Silicon Valley, recently stunned his VC colleagues with an even more extreme position, declaring that 95% of VCs add "zero value" and 80% probably "add negative value" in how they advise start-up companies in their portfolio.[3]

Whether you agree or not, the point is that you and your team need to take primary responsibility for the success/failure of your business, and that giving up excessive control to an investor can actually increase the risk of failure. And, once you accept a check, it is very difficult to say "no" to inputs from those investors.

Whenever the foundation of any relationship is not clear, the chances of upset and disappointment are greater. When you engage in investor discussions with professional investors, make it a habit to ask about their investing patterns. Find out if they typically lead the investment, whether they participate in follow-on rounds, the number of board seats that they are on, the number of investments that they have personally made, and if they are willing to help open doors. Ask, too, for specific examples that you can check out.

■ **Tip** Don't be afraid to ask pointed questions of investors. Remember, once they put money into your business, it's much like a marriage. You want to be sure you can live with the person for the long term.

What Have They Invested in Previously?

Each type of investor has their own investing strategy and habits. For example, they may only invest in certain stages of start-ups, in specific industries, in geographic locations, in graduates of a particular university—and the list goes on and on. So try to get that information before investing time in cultivating a relationship.

---

[2]*Entrepreneur*, Richard Branson, "Richard Branson on Finding and Selecting Investors for Your Startup," http://www.entrepreneur.com/article/220199, August 29, 2011.
[3]TechCrunch, Kim-Mai Cutler, "Vinod Khosla: 70-80% of VCs Add Negative Value to Startups," http://techcrunch.com/2013/09/11/vinod-khosla/, September 11, 2013.

As stated already, speak to as many companies that your prospective investors have already funded in as possible—especially the ones that didn't have loads of success. It will help you unveil what type of personality you will face when the heat turns up.

If They Invest, How Much of Your Company Do They Generally Expect to Own?

The range of ownership that investors expect to receive for their investments can vary substantially, especially in the early stages of a firm's history. A broad rule of thumb is 20% to 50% for each round. That, obviously, is a very big range. As discussed, it is important to build a spreadsheet model that shows needed capital and ownership dilution through the planned breakeven and/ or exit of the firm. You should always maintain a good understanding of what you are willing to retain at the point that your equity becomes liquid—when you can convert your paper equity to real cash. Resist giving up too much too early, since subsequent rounds may result in dilution greater than you hoped for. On the other hand, you need to be in line with the average valuations offered by investors and not be so greedy as to end up with a large ownership position and no money to go forward.

Many founders have an unrealistic view of what their percentage of ownership should be as more investment is made in their firm. Let me present a simple example. Suppose you are starting with a 40% ownership stake and that investors are willing to value your firm at $1 million (the "pre-money" valuation) prior to their investment. So you are starting with an ownership value of $400,000. You are seeking to raise an additional $1 million. After the investment is made, the "post-money" valuation is now $2 million and your ownership stake is now worth 20%. In other words, the investment has resulted in a dilution of 50% of your previous interest. This is not a bad outcome, since the added investment will now allow you to grow the firm (ideally) to much higher valuations, thereby increasing the worth of your ownership share beyond the original $400,000. (More on this in Chapter 4.)

While the actual calculations and impacts to your ownership percentage are much more complex than this simple example, you need to have a realistic view of where you end up at the point of exiting your firm (i.e., exchanging your paper equity for real cash in an IPO or acquisition transaction). It is not unusual for founders to end up with single-digit percentage ownership positions by the time their company realizes an exit. You need to be aware of this and not get overly hung up on the reduction of your ownership position, and instead focus on how to create more value from the added investments that you receive.

I am reminded of a particularly bitter experience where my venture firm had invested about $1 million in a promising early-stage semiconductor company, along with several other well-known VC firms. As we had hoped, the company took off shortly after our investment, leading a larger public company to make an offer to acquire the firm for $300 million. This would have more than met our investment objectives and created many millionaires among the founding team members. The CEO, however, believed that his firm could independently grow to $1 billion in value and refused to accept the offer—even against significant pressure from all the investors and his co-founders. Within a year, the market tanked, and the firm, along with our investment and the dreams of the founders and employees, crashed and burned.

The point of this story is to impress on you that it is generally better to accept a reasonable valuation for your efforts and move on. The CEO not only killed this deal, but he developed a poor reputation due to his poor judgment, and the consequences will likely haunt him throughout his remaining career.

In order to develop a sense of the fairness of an investment and its impact on valuation, your objective should be to obtain competing term sheets for your firm from multiple investors to help you get an idea of the appropriate market value for your current investment round. If you are stuck and cannot easily find comparable terms sheets, go back to your service providers (especially legal and accounting firms) and get their input. When interviewing service providers, consider asking, "Are you generally aware of investment terms offered to firms such as ours?" You should select at least a couple of firms that can affirmatively answer these questions. Also talk to other CEOs and see if they will share their investment terms and provide other insights that give you a better sense of the deal terms that you receive.

Lastly, be very much aware of fellow founders and key executives in your firm showing interest in knowing term sheet details. There is a fine line in determining who has a "need to know." But, once you settle on who should be in your inner circle, keep them very much in the loop and seek their advice and input—even if you really don't need it. Term sheets can have a deep emotional impact on key employees, and this is one of many areas where you need to provide both leadership and transparency.

Do They Plan to Set Aside Funds and Invest in Follow-on Rounds?

Definitely have the discussion with prospective investors about follow-on rounds of investment that may be needed to take you to at least breakeven, because whatever you think you will need to run your business for the next 12 to 24 months, you're probably wrong and will need more funds than you planned. More often than not, you will need to raise additional capital, so knowing if your current investor base has the ability to reinvest will be very useful down the road. Most professional investors will commit more capital to a firm than what is required in the current round in order to maintain their ownership position in follow-on rounds. Investors with limited resources can get "washed out" if they are unable to contribute capital in later rounds, resulting in a dilution of their ownership, and such losses can result in bad feelings about the firm and negatively impact future fundraising efforts.

Even if you have a large database of potential investors, as a general practice, target smaller groups of investors (ten or less) and close them out (i.e., get a "Yes" or "No") before moving on. Using a shotgun approach with a larger e-mail campaign can backfire, since you almost always learn something from each smaller group that will help you improve your ability to go after the next group. If you work efficiently, you can work through a longer list in a matter of just a few weeks and develop a stronger approach that will help ensure your success. Guard also against "over-shopping" your deal with intense carpet-bombing techniques, because investors prefer to look at fresh deals.

Summary

We've seen what it takes to attract and vet potential investors. The following chapters will focus on what you need to know to successfully develop an investor presentation package that will be suitable for attracting initial interest from professional investors.

Elements of this basic package include the following:

- Elevator pitch
- Executive summary
- PowerPoint
- Proof of concept/demo (if appropriate)
- References

As you move through the fundraising process, you will also need additional items, including due-diligence materials, various legal documents (e.g., a private placement memorandum), and accounting statements that will require additional investments of time and money. While there is merit to investing some time with these other "Phase II" materials, I think it is best to get your plans and concepts exposed and first generate sincere interest from bona fide investors before committing to work that may require modifications based on the feedback you receive.

Armed with the right list of target investors and these core materials, you will be prepared to deliver your story with passion, commitment, and credibility!

Venture Capital

Every year, there are about half a million businesses created in the United States, and yet less than a thousand receive venture capital funding. Although this is a low percentage, the language and concepts used by the venture capital industry have come to dominate the fundraising process, regardless of the source of capital. It is therefore very important to understand basic venture capital concepts and how VCs invest, so that you can better tailor your presentation materials to any capital source.

Venture capital is a high-risk/high-reward private equity investment, primarily in high-growth technology companies. The capital provided is in exchange for a percentage of equity (ownership) of the company, without the collateral typically required by lenders. It is important for an entrepreneur seeking venture capital to understand the history, process, and needs of the investors so that there is a good match for mutual success.

History of Venture Capital

Venture capital, a relatively new funding source, has been credited for the evolution of a large number of inventions and the development of leading new technologies and products (as well as the creation of many new jobs), which now account for about 2% of the US gross domestic product.[1] Until World War II, apart from a few wealthy families that invested and promoted selected entrepreneurs, there were limited amounts of risk capital available to start new businesses. Most available capital came in the form of personal savings or loans from friends and local banks.

---

[1]Wikipedia,"Venture capital," http://en.wikipedia.org/wiki/Venture_capital#Origins_of_modern_private_equity, 2013.

Institutional venture funds, as we see them today, started to emerge and achieve notable success beginning with firms such as Fairchild Semiconductor in 1959, and then rapidly accelerated in the 1970s as laws were relaxed, allowing pension funds to invest in VC firms. Growth continued to accelerate in the 1980s and '90s, further fueled by the increasing number of VC-funded companies that were going public (thereby providing attractive returns on VC investments) and by standardization of industry best practices and business models.

During the height of the dot-com bubble in the year 2000, there were over 2,000 VC firms in the United States alone. VC firms invested over $100 billion into start-ups in that one year. Although the number of VC firms has declined and the amount invested annually has decreased by about 70% since the peak more than 13 years ago, VC investment remains one of the most significant sources of investment capital for early-stage firms.[2]

The success of the VC capital model has affected the style and manner in which almost all investors and investment companies invest and structure deals. Even if you are not looking to raise venture capital, it is important that you study this chapter. You are sure to encounter many of the same terms and concepts, no matter what your source of capital.

The VC Business Model

Venture capital funds raise capital from large institutions, such as private equity groups, hedge funds, corporations, foreign sovereign funds, colleges and universities, public and private pension funds, family offices,[3] and so forth. Investments in venture capital funds are considered as "alternative investments" by these institutional investors. They typically commit up to 5% of the institution's investment portfolio in so-called higher-risk "alternatives, in addition to a variety of more conservative investments, such as stocks, bonds, real estate, and so forth.

Investors' main objectives for these types of investments are to take on higher risks in hopes of higher rewards that will improve the overall yield on their portfolios. The desired annualized returns from these investments are

---

[2]TechCrunch, Leena Rao, "VCs Invested $26.5B In 3,698 Companies In 2012, Total Dollars and Deal Volume Both Down," http://techcrunch.com/2013/01/17/vcs-invested-26-5b-in-3698-companies-in-2012-total-dollars-and-deal-volume-both-down/, January 17, 2013.

[3]Family offices are money-management offices that oversee investments for many wealthy families. They are often staffed with former bankers and professional wealth managers, and operate in a manner similar to other professionally managed capital sources.

typically in the range of 20% to 25%, before the funds deduct their own fees, expenses, and profit sharing.

Most venture capital funds are structured as limited liability companies owned by the investment professionals, where the investors are the limited partners (LPs), and the fund manager acts as the general partner (GP). The GP is responsible for all the day-to-day decisions regarding selection of each investment, ongoing support, reporting, and so forth. Venture capital firms typically manage multiple funds, which vary according to focus and the specific fund manager associated with a fund. These funds typically have a ten-year life, with options to extend for another two to four years if some of the investments have not been liquidated within the ten years. VC funds take a management fee of 1% to 2% of raised capital per year and also take a "carried interest" equal to 20% of the realized profits as an incentive for the fund manager.

In addition, the fund pays for any fundraising costs and the operating costs, excluding salaries for the fund managers and/or staff, rent, and so forth, which are paid by the GP. While these expenses can be significant and potentially significantly decrease the amount of actual invested capital, most funds reinvest profits to offset their expenses and come close to deploying 100% of committed capital.

The National Association of Venture Capital estimates that 40% of venture capital investments will fail, 40% will yield moderate returns, and only 20% will achieve high returns.[4] Due to these high expected-failure rates, VCs need to strive to produce very high returns, on the order of 40% to 50% IRR for each investment made, to produce acceptable net returns for the institutions whose funds they are investing.

Entrepreneurs need to be sensitive to these facts as they approach VCs. In recent years, the average returns realized by institutional investors in VC funds has dropped below the 20% to 25% IRR levels that are generally regarded as appropriate for the risk level; in fact, they have fallen to levels close to what can be obtained in the stock market—a much safer asset class. As a result, VC funds are under increasing pressure to make investments in firms that will provide home-run returns. For reference, see Figure 4-1, which shows the average returns for VC funds (compiled from a variety of sources).

---

[4]National Venture Capital Association (NVCA), http://www.nvca.org/index.php?Itemid=147.

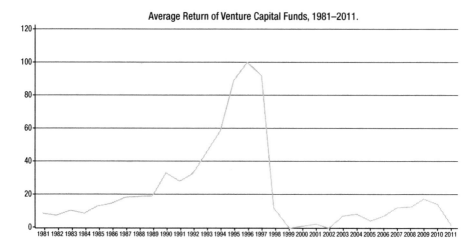

Figure 4-1. Average returns of venture capital funds[5]

VC Investment Process

The venture capital funding process comprises the following five stages of investment:

- Seed Stage (seed capital)
- Series A (start-up capital)
- Series B (early-stage capital)
- Series C (later-stage capital)
- Mezzanine (bridge capital)

These terms, along with those in the parentheses, are used both for VC and non-VC investments. Table 4-1 provides more detail.

---

[5]Based on data compiled by Cambridge Associates LLC from 1,401 US venture capital funds formed between 1981 and 2011. See *U.S. Venture Capital Index and Selected Benchmark Statistics,* June 30, 2013. Similar data is available from other sources, including the National Venture Capital Association.

Table 4-1. Overview of Financing Stages

Financing Stage	Investment Period (years)	Risk Perception	Activity to Be Financed
Seed Stage	7 to 10	Extreme	For exploring feasibility and/or early product development
Series A	5 to 9	Very high	Starting business operations and developing prototypes
Series B	3 to 7	High	Start of commercial production, marketing, and revenues
Series C	2 to 5	High	Repeat orders from larger customers, a full team in place, and predictable revenues
Mezzanine	0.5 to 2	Moderate	Prepare for IPO or acquisition

Seed Stage

Seed stage capital is generally used to explore an idea or concept. It's not meant to fund a business per se. Funds invested in this stage are for initial product development and to prove the technical and economic feasibility of a project in order to qualify for the next round of financing. The main output is to define a viable business plan that can generate satisfactory future returns for investors and, possibly, to produce a prototype or mock-up of the planned products/services.

The characteristics of the seed stage round (see Figure 4-2) can typically be described as follows:

- The company or business is established as a legal entity, along with a basic company operating agreement.
- The target product market remains general.
- The management team is not complete.
- The product or process concept is still under development.
- Intellectual property protection (patents, trade secrets) is not yet complete.
- Only the executive summary of the plan and the first version of the 12 Magic Slides are complete.

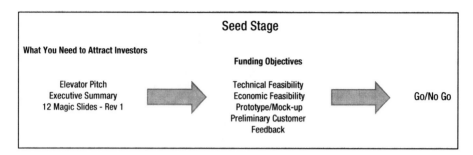

Figure 4-2. Seed stage presentation requirements and funding objectives

The first revision of your 12 magic slides emphasizes the following areas:

- Overview
- Problem
- Market
- Competitor Overview
- Founding Team
- Planned Technology
- Use of Funds and Timeline

Less content is needed for

- Marketing strategy
- Customer testimonials
- Financial road map
- Future team members

Series A Stage

Once the funding objectives of the seed stage are fully met, the next investments will be used to turn your concepts into products/services and refine your market segmentation while you continue to gain more customer validation.

The following are characteristics of the Series A stage (also see Figure 4-3):

- Filling out the executive team with suitable contributors that complement the founders. Be aware that your selection of early team members will be closely scrutinized by investors.

- Establishing the early company infrastructure, including formal planning meetings, business projections, a web site, and a place to conduct business.[6]

- Starting to monitor progress against a formal internal business plan.

- Interacting with potential customers and other validators more often.

- Testing your business model and setting initial product pricing targets.

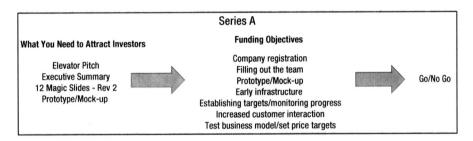

Figure 4-3. Series A presentation requirements and funding objectives

The second revision of your 12 magic slides (for the Series A financing) will emphasize the following areas:

- Overview

- Problem

- Market

- Competitor Overview

- Recent New Team Members

- Planned Technology and Prototype/Mock-up

- Use of Series A Funds and Timeline

- Basic Financial Road Map for Current and Future Rounds to Breakeven

---

[6]A growing trend for new businesses is to establish a virtual company with people working in different locations, rather than having a brick-and-mortar presence. This can be a viable approach and is acceptable to investors, provided that objectives are met and that there is accountability among team members.

Less content is needed for

- Marketing strategy
- Customer testimonials

Series B Stage

The Series B funding round typically occurs when a company has a product that can be sold to paying customers. It often follows validation of a prototype by nonpaying customers, at least some of whom are now willing to place a purchase order for a commercialized version of the product. Actual sales might be limited or merely at the order stage, but demand from paying customers can be verified—and your pricing model has at least some validation.

Since, by definition, Series B financing is associated with companies that have achieved early market success, the money is often used to hire sales and marketing people who can define an identifiable target market along with a plan of attack. They then begin to execute a sales expansion plan. The following are possible characteristics of a Series B financing stage:

- Having a product or service that credible customers are willing to pay for.
- Generating little or no sales revenue.
- Spending more than you take in; no profits.
- Creating a plan to complete the management team, and hiring sales, marketing, and finance people who have proven experience in growing similar businesses to profitability.
- Validating expectations through increased customer feedback and near-term substantial growth in revenue and profits.

The third revision of your 12 magic slides (for the Series B financing) should have compelling content for all slides—with further customer validation to be added as available.

This stage (see Figure 4-4) may take as long as four to six years to be realized—or it could happen much faster. Evidence of this stage can be seen when the company has a fully assembled management team and a marketable product.

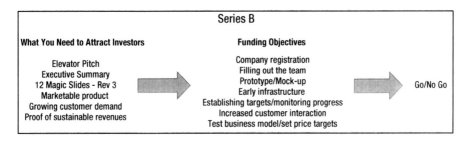

Figure 4-4. Series B presentation requirements and funding objectives

Companies seek Series B financing because

- Series A capital has been exhausted on product development.

- The demand curve for product has now reached a point where additional personnel need to be hired to realize initial market success.

- You are able to offer evidence of future sustainable revenues, although breakeven and profitability may remain speculative.

Venture capitalists who have previously invested in the firm are very likely to participate in this Series B round, but a new VC lead investor may be asked to participate in order to objectively set appropriate terms and conditions for valuing the investment at this stage. At this stage, capital needs are the greatest—and the firm has still not developed any appreciable cash flow.

This funding round is arguably the sweet spot for The 12 Magic Slides presentation, because you will need to pull out all the stops to ensure the survival of the business.

Firms at this stage face a couple of risks. First, you may become known to larger, better-capitalized competition. They may try to muscle in and seize the market opportunity. Second, there's always the risk of product obsolescence, because larger firms may have also seen similar market opportunities and released products that will be more attractive to your target customers.

Series C Stage

Series C funding is also an expansion round, because funds raised will typically be disproportionately used for marketing and for meeting the working capital needs of a company that has now established production and has revenue.

But the company does not have sufficient positive cash flows to take full advantage of the potential market opportunity.

The following are characteristics of a Series C stage:

- Products on the market

- Management team in place

- Sales revenue being generated from one or more product lines

- Repeat orders from large customers

- Growing brand awareness in market niche

- The company is still losing money or just breaking even at this stage, so external funds are still required to fund growth

The fourth revision of your 12 magic slides (for the Series C financing) should have compelling content for all slides, with added customer validation and more details on the total funds needed to realize an exit for the investor (i.e., the full return of invested capital plus profits).

Series C financing generally occurs at the point the firm's business model has been fully validated (see Figure 4-5). How do you know when this has been accomplished? First, the business model of a firm comprises all the significant factors that combine to generate revenues and increase profits. The components of a business model can include:

- Pricing

- Manufacturing and delivery processes

- Distribution strategy

- Cost of producing your products/services

- Labor costs

- Evidence that you can defend your niche against competition

- Comparisons to competition

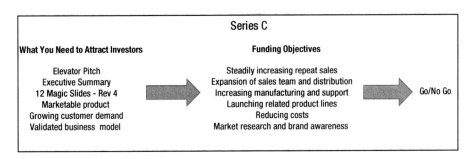

Figure 4-5. Series C presentation requirements and funding objectives

To validate a business model means that you have developed solutions for all of these items, and you have tested them repeatedly and confirmed that your revenues and profits can be sustained and/or improved.

Series C lead investors are typically looking to have an exit in three to seven years, and they will need to see financial projections that fit this time frame in your funding presentation.

Mezzanine

Mezzanine, or bridge financing, is the final round of investment sought before a planned IPO or a likely acquisition of the firm by a larger company (see Figure 4-6). It is the last round of financing. Many times, companies at this stage are already profitable, but they still seek outside capital to improve their balance sheets. This can increase their valuation. The lead investor in this round often assists the firm by

- Setting a value on the firm's pre-public stock, which sets the stage for the firm's value at the time of IPO or acquisition.

- Assisting the firm to select and interact with investment bankers and other intermediaries (e.g., accountants, analysts, market makers, etc.) that will be required to complete the contemplated transaction.

- Providing critical input on the completion of required documents for the planned exit (e.g., SEC filing statements, disclosures, etc.).

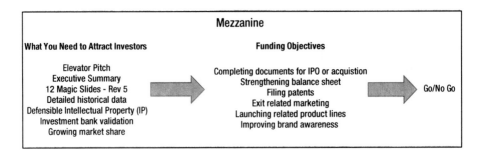

Figure 4-6. Mezzanine presentation requirements and funding objectives

Investors who invest at the mezzanine stage typically expect to exit the investment within 6 to 24 months. Since the time frame at this investment stage is shorter and the overall company risks are lower, the required returns to investors are lower than that for the investors who participated in the earlier rounds.

In order to attract suitable mezzanine stage investors, you will need to provide the following:

- A funding presentation focusing on the historical accomplishments and external validation of potential value at the time of IPO or acquisition (The 12 Magic Slides with updates)

- Detailed historical data

- Proof of solid barriers against potential competition (patents, trade secrets, "secret sauce")

- External validation of potential value at the time of IPO or acquisition

- Evidence of growing brand awareness and market share in your target market

VC Investment Criteria

Although venture capital investors are the most rigorous of all the investors you are likely to encounter, their criteria for investing are generally the same as other investor types. Venture capital investors are looking for the following in a company:

- Exponential growth potential

- An attractive industry

- A sustainable business model validated by paying customers
- Excellent team "execution" that delivers on your expectations
- Founders who are willing to act on input from outside investors
- Owners willing to share wealth
- A credible exit plan within four to seven years

The 12 Magic Slides process will help you nail these hot buttons!

Typical IRR Requirements

Due to multiple factors, VCs demand very high returns or IRR (see Chapter 1) compared to other investments.

Management fees and profit sharing. Due to management fees and profit sharing, the percentage of actual funds committed to investments may be less than the total funds raised. Returns, therefore, must be higher.

A long holding period. As I have shown, IRR is greatly influenced by the amount of time required to pay back both invested capital and all profits. VCs need to plan for returns not being realized for five to ten years. That raises the bar on required returns.

A low success rate. It is common that as many as 40% of the investments made by each fund will be outright failures, and about 40% will breakeven, leaving 20% to actually deliver the full expected returns for the entire fund. If you are lucky enough to have a company like Facebook among your fund investments, you can tolerate a lot of failures and still be a hero to your investors. Such deals, however, can only be evaluated using a rearview mirror. So the pressure is to realize high returns on all deals, even when you may have a big winner (and I want to emphasize "may have" since nothing is certain).

No liquidity options. Investments made by VC funds are considered illiquid because there are very few options for investors to sell their interests to others prior to an exit. So once you're in, you need to consider that you're in for the long haul. Not unlike other venture funds, my own investment fund has some deals that we continue to manage up to 14 years after our original investment was made! So we now look for deals that we can exit in five years or less, understanding that some may take much longer.

No assets to secure investments. VCs invest cash (equity); generally, cash or equity carries the highest amount of risk because they are unsecured against any significant collateral. If the company fails, its assets will be liquidated and the proceeds will go to holders of debt ahead of those who have equity. This is why loans can be arranged at a lower cost of capital and why equity requires a much higher return.

Table 4-2 shows typical IRR requirements for VC investments, which entrepreneurs need to be cognizant of when presenting their business plans to VCs for funding.

Table 4-2. The Returns Investors Look for at Each Round of Investing

Investment Round	Expected IRR
Seed Stage	60% to 80%
Series A	50% to 70%
Series B	40% to 60%
Series C	30% to 50%
Mezzanine	20% to 35%

Investment Multiples Required (Cash on Cash)

As discussed in Chapter 1, many investors discuss their required returns in terms of "cash on cash" or as a multiple of cash received vs. cash invested. While this comparison overlooks the time value of money (i.e., cash returned sooner is better than the same amount of cash being returned later), it is still very common to hear investors discuss returns in these terms. So, for example, you might hear somebody say, "I got 5X on that deal."

Table 4-3 compares required investment multiples to expected IRR returns, with total funds returned after three years, five years, and ten years.

Table 4-3. Cash Multiples as compared to IRR

Investment	IRR %	Years	Multiple
$1M	35%	3	2.5
$1M	50%	3	3.4
$1M	80%	3	5.8
$1M	35%	5	4.9
$1M	50%	5	7.6
$1M	80%	5	18.9
$1M	35%	10	20.1
$1M	50%	10	57.7
$1M	80%	10	357.0

Note that if your company cannot realize a full exit (i.e., return of all invested funds) until ten years from the investment date, the expected multiples go to stratospheric levels! That is why investors will seldom consider investments that do not project a full return of all capital and profits within five years. That is not to say that you should be dishonest and skew your business plan to show a five-year return, because this will likely be discovered by astute investors in any case.

As always, dishonesty is a career killer—and you need to avoid any temptations that may take you there. It's better to find ways to improve your business model to realistically project returns than to be intentionally deceitful.

Typical Equity Investment Structures

The final—and arguably the most important—consideration in evaluating VC capital is to be aware of how much of your firm you may be asked to give up in return for the capital sought. Table 4-4 provides some insight. These numbers are averages that I have seen across many deals; they are not cast in concrete. While each deal is unique, in general, you can expect to give up greater amounts of your ownership interests in earlier rounds. The first external capital that you seek will also be much more likely to cost you 40% to 50%—than, say, 10% to 20% later on.

Table 4-4. Typical Amounts of Ownership Interests Sold in Each Financing Stage

Stage	Amount Sought	Pre-Money Valuation	% Ownership Sold
Seed	$1M to $2M	$1.5M to $5M	40% to 50%
Series A	$3M to $5M	$5M to $8M	30% to 50%
Series B	$5M to $10M	$15M to $30M	20% to 30%
Series C	$15M to $20M	$50M to $60M	15% to 20%
Bridge to IPO	$10M to $20M	$100M to $200M	10% to 15%

This chart may shock some of you, but the reality is that while it is expensive in terms of your ownership to attract outside capital, it is the way the investment world works—and you need to get comfortable with decline in your personal ownership.

Note the term *pre-money valuation* in Table 4-4. It is an important term to understand. It is the agreed-upon, hoped-for value of a company prior to the next round of funding. Post-money valuation, on the other hand, is the value of the firm, including the new outside financing.

Here are several examples that should help you understand these concepts and the implications of changes of ownership value (i.e., "dilution").

Let's assume that you have organized your firm[7] and issued one million shares. Prior to seeking outside investment, you would own 100% of the company. However, the value and share price of your company is not worth much at this stage. It is indeterminate[8] because you do not have any external validation to set an objective value (Note that your opinion of the value of your company is not worth much at this stage!). Table 4-5 summarizes your starting position.

Table 4-5. Ownership Interests Prior to External Investment

Stock Holders	Investment Amount	Pre-Money Valuation	Price per Share	Number of Shares Issued	Post-Money Valuation	Number of Shares Owned	Ownership Percentage
Company	Sweat Equity	N/A	N/A	1,000,000	N/A	1,000,000	100%

[7]This means that you have properly incorporated and registered your firm with appropriate legal documents. Firms typically begin by authorizing a large amount of stock—let's say 10,000,000 shares—and then issue new stock from this larger authorized pool that is sold to new investors.
[8]Your incorporation documents will typically state a stock value of $.01 or $.001 per share. But these values are meaningless unless validated by outside investment.

You now decide to raise your first external capital and have found seed investors who are willing to invest $1,000,000 at a post-money[9] valuation of $2,000,000, at a price of $1.00 per share. Table 4-6 shows how your ownership position will change.

Table 4-6. Ownership Interests After Seed Round

Stock Holders	Investment Amount	Pre-Money Valuation	Price per Share	Number of New Shares Issued	Post-Money Valuation	Number of Shares Owned	Ownership Percentage
Company			$1.00		$1,000,000	1,000,000	50%
Seed Investors	$1,000,000	$1,000,000	$1.00	1,000,000	$1,000,000	1,000,000	50%
Total				**1,000,000**	**$2,000,000**	**2,000,000**	

Although your ownership has gone down by 50%, you now own 50% of a company that has been valued by outside investors at $2,000,000. And, most importantly, you now have the needed capital to grow your firm to the next stage. This is a good outcome!

Let's go further and now presume you are ready to raise your Series A round and have found investors who will pay you $3.00 per share and invest $3,000,000 on a $6,000,000 pre-money valuation due to the increased value that you created with capital from the seed round. Table 4-7 shows how your ownership position will change.

Table 4-7. Ownership Interests After Series A Round

Stock Holders	Investment Amount	Pre-Money Valuation	Price per Share	Number of New Shares Issued	Post-Money Valuation	Number of Shares Owned	Ownership Percentage
Company			$3.00		$3,000,000	1,000,000	33%
Seed Investors			$3.00		$3,000,000	1,000,000	33%
Series A Investors	3,000,000	$6,000,000	$3.00	1,000,000	$3,000,000	1,000,000	33%
Total				**1,000,000**	**$9,000,000**	**3,000,000**	

---

[9]The term "post-money" is commonly used to describe the value of firm after an investment is made.

The total amount of issued stock increases to 3,000,000 shares and at a post-money valuation of $9,000,000, the value of your ownership position increases to $3,000,000. So now the value of your personal stake has increased, even though the percentage has gone down—and you have a fresh slug of new capital to grow your business even further. More good news!

Similarly, should you seek a B round at some point; it might look like Table 4-8.

Table 4-8. Ownership Interests After Series B Round

Stock Holders	Investment Amount	Pre-Money Valuation	Price per Share	Number of New Shares Issued	Post-Money Valuation	Number of Shares Owned	Ownership Percent
Company			$5.00		$5,000,000	1,000,000	25%
Seed Investors			$5.00		$5,000,000	1,000,000	25%
Series A Investors			$5.00		$5,000,000	1,000,000	25%
Series B Investors	5,000,000	$15,000,000	$5.00	1,000,000	$5,000,000	1,000,000	25%
Total				1,000,000	$20,000,000	4,000,000	

Now the value of your stake has grown to 25% of the $20,000,000—or $5,000,000.

Although the foregoing examples are vastly simplified using rosy growth and value assumptions,[10] this is indicative of what entrepreneurs experience in a successful, growing business. And, hopefully, you now understand why you should not get overly hung up on giving up ownership stakes to raise needed growth capital. Make sure this sinks in.

Tip Think of your ownership dilution as a way to increase your wealth, not decrease it—because if you are successful, this will be the outcome.

---

[10]One of the many simplifications made here was to assume the prior investors would not invest in future rounds and also experience a decrease in their ownership position. In reality, prior investors typically invest more money in each round at prices set by the new external investor.

This discussion is very introductory, and there are many more details and tradeoffs that CEOs must understand to provide effective leadership on related investment negotiations. In particular, I encourage you to invest further time learning about capital structures and governance matters.

Many inexperienced entrepreneurs tend to focus more on the capital raised and the related dilution of their interests. However, the terms of VC investments also include provisions that can significantly impact otherwise attractive valuation terms. Even if you possess prior experience in evaluating these areas, you should seek advice from an experienced finance person or a qualified attorney since there can often be "devils in the details" that can come back to catch unwary founders.

Summary

The venture capital industry has dramatically influenced the manner in which all investors invest. Even though relatively few firms receive VC funds, the investment process—no matter who the investor is—is guided by the same general principles, terms, and conditions that have been developed by VCs. As an entrepreneur, you must understand at least the basic concepts outlined in this chapter. You must also make sure that your financial projections generally achieve the returns that your target investors are seeking.

Due to the costs associated with supporting a VC fund, the returns that you produce for VCs must be higher than that for other types of investors, who may have less overhead and profit-sharing costs to offset to obtain their desired outcome.

While obtaining VC financing can be very challenging, especially from top-tier funds, the benefits can be substantial. Having a good VC investor aboard will provide strong validation for your business, help you attract other investors and top service providers, and improve your ability to land top employees.

That is not to say that you fold your tent if you cannot land VC capital. VCs focus on high-risk, high-reward opportunities. If your business is lower risk and provides moderate returns, you are still very likely to find investors that match your business profile. Not every investor is looking for high-risk investments, after all.

Another important and nonintuitive concept for many new entrepreneurs is to understand how ownership changes as external investments are made. I have seen many good ideas that fail to obtain funding because the founders are unwilling to give up the required ownership to attract new investors. A common saying among successful entrepreneurs is: "It is not what you start with, but what you end up with."

Realize that there are many billionaires who have only single-digit ownership of their firms—and would not have been able to get there without external capital and the related dilution. My advice to you is to "eat when served" and take needed capital on fair terms, and move on to focus on growing your business.

In all cases, the terms and concepts in this chapter apply to all types of investors, so take the time to make sure you thoroughly understand this material.

Now that you have a better idea of what investors are looking for and how they think and consider deals, it is time to take your first steps to building your killer presentation. In the following chapters, I will break down this process, step by step, starting with the next chapter, which includes a proven approach to getting investors interested in meeting with you and hearing more about your company.

The Elevator Pitch

The first and perhaps most important tool in your presentation materials is the *elevator pitch*. In its most simple terms, an elevator pitch is a brief summary of your business that is developed to entice an investor to want to hear more. It is short enough to be told as you ride in an elevator with a prospective investor. Hence the name.

The elevator pitch is the first step in getting a check from investors. It can also be repurposed to achieve other important objectives, including:

- Attracting new employees
- Gaining new customers
- Getting a bank loan
- Hiring a new service provider
- Networking with other entrepreneurs

The elevator pitch will be used more often than any of your other materials and is critical in establishing a positive first impression. The objective is to create interest in learning more about your firm—quickly, clearly, and distinctly to someone you have not previously met. Creating a good pitch is not easy and requires ongoing refinement and practice so that you can deliver it quickly, on the spot, and under pressure.

Look at it this way: every entrepreneur has an answer to the question "What does your company do?" The answer to that question becomes an elevator pitch when...

- The objective is to secure interest in what you do and lead to desired next steps with investors, clients, employees, and partners—people who may have a positive financial impact on your business.

- You are engaged in a professional conversation that may lead to introductions to others who can help you achieve your business objectives.

- You want to create a lasting impression on an individual who will help develop image and brand awareness for your offerings.

THE PURPOSE OF AN ELEVATOR PITCH

Elevator pitches are used to

- Get first meetings with investors.

- Create interest in learning more.

- Provide a rallying point for internal strategy.

- Demonstrate clear understanding about the important parts of your story.

- Optimize use of limited time to make an impression.

- Ensure that everyone on your team is on the same page.

Of course, the most powerful use is to secure a meeting with an investor who can fund your business.

Variations of elevator pitches are not only used in verbal communication, but they can and should be used in written correspondence. They may also be appropriate for use in marketing collateral, including web sites, advertising, and so forth.

While there is no "one size fits all" formula for the perfect elevator pitch, there are a number of best practices. In an elevator pitch, it is important to do the following:

- Keep it short—60 seconds or less

- Open with a "wow" factor that describes urgent pain and sets an immediate hook to capture interest

- Let the listeners know what you are ultimately seeking from them (money, referral, etc.)

- Establish your expertise and credibility

- Exude confidence, passion, and enthusiasm, and punctuate with appropriate body gestures

- Keep it slow—speak no faster than about 200 words per minute (time it with the stopwatch on your smartphone)

- Speak deliberately and clearly, and make appropriate eye contact (when face to face)

- Make every word count

- Use vocabulary that the listener will understand and that establishes your expertise and credibility

- Close with a question or a call to action to draw the listener into the conversation and gain buy-in

This chapter will help you understand why it's important to do these things—and how to do them effectively.

Short vs. Long Format

There are two common formats for an elevator pitch: short form (30 seconds) and long form (60 seconds). During workshops that were delivered by my investment banking firm, Venture Navigation, we focused on first developing a long-form pitch and then whittling it down into a short form. We found that it was difficult to do a short form until the key ideas in a good long-form pitch were developed.

The short form of the elevator pitch is appropriate for certain situations, such as when you are unsure your listener has any interest in your space. This shorter form is typically the first 30 to 40 words of your longer elevator pitch and consists of your basic business summary.

Although you will end up using the short-form pitch more often, the long form is more commonly used for investors who are looking to hear a little more about your company than other groups. So let's start with the long form.

The maximum length of the long-form elevator pitch should be about 200 words, which can be verbally presented—comfortably—in about 60 seconds. Especially in these post-Twitter days, when more and more people communicate using fewer and fewer words, count on having only 30 to 60 seconds to gain investor interest, or you can count on losing them forever. If your pitch is longer, you are crossing into territory that should be saved for your follow-on presentation—and you will likely lose, not gain, interest from your listener.

Through seeing reactions to hundreds of elevator pitches, I believe 60 seconds has proved to be the ideal length of your monologue to investors before giving the listener an opportunity to speak. Investors tend to get uneasy at the 60-second mark and visibly begin to tune out what is being said. (But you will gain interest and score critical buy-in points by engaging your listener with a closing question or two to allow them to express their initial impression of what you have shared.)

In considering which points to emphasize, consider the following hierarchy of possible benefits that you provide to customers:

- You help your customers generate more revenue (e.g., a stock trading program)
- You save costs (e.g., a lower-cost substitute)
- You create efficiencies (e.g., a new manufacturing machine)
- You make them healthier (e.g., a new drug)
- You make them more skillful (e.g., a new golf club)
- You increase their sense of prestige (e.g., a Rolex watch)
- You allow them to do something in a different way (e.g., an iPhone newspaper app)

Take an objective look at your planned product offering and determine its highest and best possible benefit to your target customer. As suggested by this hierarchy, build your short-form elevator pitch around the highest benefit(s) that you deliver.

The best approach is to start by first understanding the most valuable benefit you provide, and then to compose a series of short bullets covering your most impactful opening talking points. Put this aside for a day or so, and then come back and determine the points that would be most likely to hook a potential investor in less than 60 seconds, starting with your most powerful points.

Once that is done, you now not only have a good start on your long-form pitch, you also have developed an attention-grabbing introduction that can be an effective short-form pitch.

Ironically, through the countless interactions with entrepreneurs in our workshops, we have seen that it is more difficult to compose a short-form elevator pitch than a longer one. Once you have a compelling long-form pitch, determine the most compelling two points and you will be well on your way to a good short-form pitch.

Note   Your short version should also incorporate an answer to the two basic questions that anyone would likely ask: What does your company do? (Start with highest benefit you provide: "We generate more money for companies that advertise on the Internet..."). Who are your customers? ("We are targeting real estate companies, including agents and brokers selling single-family homes...").

And, of course, the long version is the one you really want to give to investors, since it makes the points that will excite them when you just happen to be riding that elevator up to the top floor with him.

Creating Impactful Content

During our many workshops with entrepreneurs over the years, we found that the creation of a good elevator pitch was often surprisingly stressful and frequently produced heated disagreements among team members. One factor that contributed to differing approaches was a lack of understanding the pitch's goal. The sole objective of this pitch—unlike those designed, perhaps, to land a job interview or to meet and impress a new social friend—is to create interest in learning more about your business and getting the listener to voluntarily commit the time to learn more about your firm as a potential investment.

We found that it was very helpful to have investors listen to newly developed pitches in our workshops, and then provide feedback to CEOs by using the following eight criteria and ranking each presentation on a scale of 1 to 10:

- Urgent pain, generation of new revenue, or significant performance improvement
- Clearly define your product/solution
- Large, growing market
- Evidence of your expertise
- Unique, defensible position
- Validation
- Communication skills
- Call to action/desire to hear more

Before presenting specific examples, let's examine each of these areas in more detail.

Urgent Pain, New Revenue, or Performance Improvement

A "wow" factor that cites a serious and meaningful problem that customers are experiencing, or a claim of significant performance improvement in an area that matters to many people, can create a good opener. The following are a few examples:

- Increasing the ability of your customers to make more money

- Diagnosing and/or curing significant problems (and cite impact on health, premature failure, excess cost and time, deteriorating conditions)

- Describing significant performance improvements (speed, power, aesthetics, longevity)

Define Your Product or Service

It is most effective if you describe your product/service as a solution to a significant problem. The following are possible examples:

- "We have developed a solution to allow early detection of arterial disease that is far more accurate than any current tests."

- "Our battery technology will double the range of an electric car."

- "The noise cancellation technology that we have developed can be used in a wide range of products—from headphones to automobiles, and even airline cabins, to provide an ultra-quiet listening experience that is superior to anything on the market."

Large, Growing Market

Investors who are investing in riskier technology firms will often not consider firms unless they are tackling markets of $1 billion or more. Smaller markets can be attractive if they are rapidly growing and/or you are able to offer ongoing cash flow (e.g., dividends or debt service payments) to speed up returns.

Evidence of Your Expertise

Once you have your listener's attention, it's time to establish that you are knowledgeable in your area by providing some evidence of your expertise; for example, "This is a spin-off of my last company, which I successfully took public and then sold to Cisco for $1 billion," or "I have a PhD in physics from MIT and I have filed numerous patents in this field," or (less desirably) "I have studied this area for five years and I have attracted a top team of industry experts."

Unique, Defensible Position

What is to stop someone from taking your idea and putting you out of business? In an investor elevator pitch, the short form of this answer is to simply declare that you have a "unique," "protected," "proprietary," and/or "patented" solution, which implies that you have established some barriers to competition.

Validation

Cite customers, partners, and/or other investors who have evaluated and committed to your offerings.

Communication Skills

The way you deliver your pitch is likely to be more memorable than your content. So make sure that you appear confident, passionate, and smart, and show off some of your CEO star power.

Call to Action

Often forgotten, the call to action is critical to a successful pitch. It can be a simple leading question such as: "Do you want to hear more?" or "Would you like me to send you more information?" or "Is this area something that might fit your investment objectives?"

A great elevator pitch is only as good as the call to action. And if you have successfully pulled off establishing a good perception of the points leading up to your call to action (and presuming that investor has a general interest in your sector), you will be rewarded with a "Yes" to these types of questions. If your next step cannot be taken immediately, be sure to exchange contact information and follow up promptly to schedule next steps, preferably then and there ("How about this Thursday at 10 a.m.?").

Optional Areas

There are several optional areas that can be effectively included to make your elevator pitch more compelling.

Competition and Differentiators

Comments about having no competitors are best avoided. If you are in a crowded market, it's best to acknowledge the obvious and add a comment on why you will win.

Revenue Model

Since the arrival of the Internet, there has been an explosion in creative and new revenue models for companies. If your revenue model is an important differentiator, make sure you mention it in your elevator pitch.

Investment Required, Use of Funds, and Payback Estimate

I generally think a discussion of these items is best left to a follow-on discussion where you can share more information and learn more about the appetite of the investor. There are times, however, when it makes sense to include in your elevator pitch some introductory comments related to the investment amount; for example, "We are seeking a $1.5 million investment to fund manufacturing, marketing, and initial product distribution. Within five years, we seek to achieve an IPO, at which time investors can expect a payback at about a 20% ROI." (Although, without more information about the company, any sophisticated investor will view this last sentence with a great deal of skepticism.)

Tip Keep the objective of the elevator pitch in mind: to land a follow-up meeting. The elevator pitch is not meant to substitute for a more detailed PowerPoint presentation or business plan—so slim it down to what is needed to get the investor to commit to next steps. A bloated pitch (which too many are) is very likely to produce a negative first impression. It's much better to create interest to learn more than to strive to explain all.

Elevator Pitch Examples: Understanding What Works and What Doesn't[1]

Now that you know what should be included in a successful elevator pitch, let's study and analyze some examples. These all show different degrees of adherence to the criteria that I laid out. I am omitting discussion of the communication skills of each presenter because you don't have the benefit of seeing them in action, but this is a very critical area and should be evaluated when developing your pitch or critiquing others.

The examples are presented in order from best to worst so that you can get a better sense of how the critical points need to be addressed to achieve your goal of follow-on interest.

Example 1: DiamondWerks

DiamondWerks develops proprietary, thin-film diamond products and equipment that dramatically improve heat dissipation on microprocessors, solving one of the highest-priority pain points in the industry. Without a solution such as ours, improvements in computer performance will dramatically decline. We address rapidly growing markets that will exceed $1.5 billion by 2016, and we will become the dominant supplier.

I have previously started and sold two successful companies in this field for over $500 million. I have assembled the best team in the industry and I have the most comprehensive patent position of any company in this field. [Fortune 100 company] is our largest current investor and is evaluating our products for use in their next high-performance microprocessors. We are actively engaged with other top target customers and partners, who will provide very strong references.

We are seeking $3 million to help us expand our manufacturing capabilities to meet demand and to get to breakeven within the next 12 months.

Is this an area that your firm would consider making an investment? Would you like me to send you more information?

Review this pitch against the following criteria.

What urgent problem are you solving?

> *"[Our products] dramatically improve heat dissipation on microprocessors, solving one of the highest-priority pain points in the industry."*

---

[1] The examples are drawn from real company pitches, however, details have been modified to emphasize certain points and to protect confidentiality.

Clearly define your product/solution.

> *"DiamondWerks develops proprietary, thin-film diamond products and equipment."*

Large, growing market?

> *"We address rapidly growing markets that will exceed $1.5 billion by 2016."*

Your expertise?

> *"I have previously started and sold two successful companies in this field for over $500 million."*

Unique, defensible position?

> *"I have the best team in the industry and the most comprehensive patent position of any company."*

Validation?

> *"[Fortune 100 company] is our largest current investor... We are actively engaged with other top target customers and partners who provide very strong references."*

Call to action?

> *"Is this an area that your firm would consider making an investment? Would you like me to send you more information?"*

Comments

This pitch scored a perfect 10 out of 10 in all eight criteria from investors attending our workshops. It has all the elements that should be modeled to attract investor interest in next steps. It also included one of the optional criteria mentioned—the amount of investment being sought and its purpose. All within a modest 179 words that can be presented in well under one minute.

Example II: Apostle Networks

Apostle Networks is a leading supplier of wireless access solutions. We provide a breakthrough solution to one of today's critical network bottlenecks—limited availability of last-mile broadband access to millions of prospective users worldwide. Apostle's patent-pending PacketFlo system provides a range of products that dramatically increase performance for both new and existing broadband deployments and addresses one of the fastest-growing segments of the multibillion-dollar broad-band market. We have growing revenues and a prestigious list of customers, including Honey Networks and Sentash Technologies, among others.

After receiving my PhD in electrical engineering from MIT, I was a successful technologist in firms such as Ares Corporation and IBC Research Center, and became Vice President of Engineering at LanVision. I have been awarded eight patents in networking-related technology areas.

We are seeking $10 million in order to complete our next product launch and position our firm for an IPO or acquisition within 24 months. I am very familiar with your firm's prior investments in this area. I would be pleased to further discuss how an investment in Apostle Networks would be complementary to your investment portfolio. Are you available for a follow-up meeting next Tuesday?

Let's take a deeper look at this one against our criteria.

What urgent problem are you solving?

"We provide a breakthrough solution to one of today's critical network bottlenecks—limited availability of last-mile broadband access to millions of prospective users worldwide."

Clearly define your product/solution.

"Apostle Networks is a leading supplier of wireless access solutions."

Large, growing market?

"[We] address one of the fastest-growing segments of the multibillion-dollar broadband market."

Your expertise?

"After receiving my PhD in electrical engineering from MIT I was a successful technologist in firms such as Ares Corporation *and* IBC Research Center, *and became* Vice President of Engineering at LanVision. *I have been awarded eight patents in networking-related technology areas."*

Unique, defensible position?

"Apostle's patent-pending PacketFlo system…"

Validation?

"We have growing revenues and a prestigious list of customers, including Honey Networks and Sentash Technologies, among others."

Call to action?

"I am very familiar with your firm's prior investments in this area. I would be pleased to further discuss how an investment in Apostle Networks would be complementary to your investment portfolio Are you available for a follow-up meeting next Tuesday?"

Comments

Although this elevator pitch hits all the key areas, our evaluators suggested that more work and polish was needed. The market needed to be better defined and more information about the barriers to entry needed to be included. Unlike DiamondWerks, Apostle Networks was known to have many competitors with various other ways to solve the "last mile" problem. The call to action was especially powerful, since the CEO was a well-recognized expert in networking technology and many investors would welcome his input on similar technology investments; so he took advantage of this to get more time to present his complete story.

The overall ranking against the 8 criteria was an 8 out of 10.

Example III: Inamay

Have you ever wanted to use your cell phone on an airplane? We provide an FAA-approved system that is the first of its type to allow cell phones to work on airplanes equipped with Wi-Fi. This is a very large and rapidly growing market since more and more airplanes are becoming enabled with Wi-Fi. Our system allows both airlines and cell phone providers such as AT&T and Verizon to generate additional revenues. The market size in the United States alone is expected to exceed $3 billion within five years, and the international market is estimated to be four times larger. Our technology is protected with several pending patents and, along with our first-mover advantage, we have a significant lead over potential competitors. We provide free installation of our system and generate revenues from each call that is made.

We are seeking a $2.3 million investment to fund the development of our first systems, complete the filing of our initial patent portfolio, and to start trials with a major airline. Within five years, we plan to IPO the firm, and investors can expect to realize at least a 10X return on their investment.

What urgent problem are you solving?

"Have you ever wanted to use you cell phone on an airplane?"

Clearly define your product/solution.

"We provide an FAA-approved system that is the first of its type to allow cell phones to work on airplanes equipped with Wi-Fi."

Large, growing market?

"The market size in the United States alone is expected to exceed $3 billion within five years, and the international market is estimated to be four times larger."

Your expertise?

This entrepreneur omits discussing this and effectively shoots himself in the foot. After hearing many good pitches where CEOs and founders proudly discuss their accomplishments, investors will conclude that a pitch that omits solid relevant experience is very likely an indication that this CEO lacks the requisite background to land an investment.

Competition and differentiators.

"Our technology is protected with several pending patents, and along with our first-mover advantage, we have a significant advantage over potential competitors."

Revenue model.

"We provide free installation of our system and generate revenues from each call that is made."

Investment required and payback estimate.

"We are seeking a $2.3 million investment to fund the development of our first systems, to complete the filing of our initial patent portfolio, and to start trials with a major airline. Within five years, we plan to IPO the firm, and investors can expect to realize at least a 10X return on their investment."

Call to action?

None.

Comments

Failure to mention relevant background and experience, as well as not delivering a strong call for action to obtain a meeting, are glaring faults with this pitch. Although most key criteria points were touched on, I present this example to demonstrate that **80%** correct does not get the job done. Make sure you speak to all the identified areas and always close with a call to action.

Overall ranking against our criteria was 6 out of 10.

Example IV: SportCloz.com

Our company is called SportCloz.com, and we are an e-commerce web site that sells high-quality, custom-fitted uniforms to amateur and professional athletes at highly competitive prices. Utilizing a supply chain that we are creating, which extends to Asia, we are able to offer high-quality, custom uniforms at up to 70% less than comparable firms—and make them available in as little as ten days after an order has been placed. We also plan to utilize a proprietary smartphone app that can quickly determine precise measurements through taking four pictures of each customer, which are then immediately uploaded to our cloud-based servers, processed, and sent to our manufacturing sites within seconds.

There are currently no firms that target professional and amateur athletes in a similar manner—and none that have our ability to quickly and precisely take measurements via smartphones. SportCloz.com has a growing number of agreements with amateur sports teams and is currently in discussion with the NFL to begin sales to professional football players. These groups will promote our site to their players and also provide us with joint advertising opportunities on other sites that feature their brands and logos.

In our market surveys, over 90% of amateur and professional athletes have expressed strong interest in buying custom-made uniforms that fit well and are less expensive than those currently available. The market for our products is well over $1 billion. We need $1.8 million in funding to get to breakeven. This should happen within two years. Right now, we're seeking a seed round of $500,000 in exchange for 25% ownership in the company.

I am a CEO with lots of operational experience and deep contacts with amateur and professional sports teams. Our Sales VP led the growth and eventual sale of an online custom clothing company to Joseph Banks. If we can close on our financing this year, we expect to be able to sell SportCloz.com to a major clothing firm within three years.

Let's evaluate this last example.

What urgent problem are you solving?

> *"[We] are able to offer high-quality, custom uniforms at up to 70% less than comparable firms—and make them available in as little as ten days after an order has been placed."*

Clearly define your product/solution.

"[We sell] high-quality, custom-fitted uniforms to amateur and professional athletes at highly competitive prices."

Large, growing market?

"The market for our products is well over $1 billion."

Your expertise?

"I am a CEO with lots of operational experience and deep contacts with amateur and professional sports teams. Our Sales VP led the growth and eventual sale of an online custom clothing company to Joseph Banks."

Unique, defensible position?

"There are currently no firms that target professional and amateur athletes in a similar manner—and none that have our ability to quickly and precisely take measurements via smartphones."

Validation?

"SportCloz.com has a growing number of agreements with amateur sports teams and is currently in discussion with the NFL to begin sales to professional football players."

Investment required and payback estimate.

"Right now, we're seeking a seed round of $500,000 in exchange for 25% ownership in the company."

Call to action?

None.

Comments

In spite of a somewhat good start, this pitch does not make the grade. While the stated differentiators are interesting (a supply chain and an app to take measurements), they come across as "futures" that have yet to be completed differentiators. The payback estimate is uncertain, there is no explanation of use of funds, and most glaringly, no call to action (not that any call for this one would elicit a favorable response). Finally, it's too long. The elevator would have reached the ground floor and the potential investor would have walked off two-thirds of the way through the pitch.

Overall rating against our criteria: 5 out of 10.

How to Develop a Compelling Elevator Pitch

First, reread this chapter several times and study the examples thoroughly. Start developing your own elevator pitch by writing down all the criteria discussed, including the optional areas. Then write down short bullets that apply to each area without overly thinking about the exact words that you may ultimately use. The objective is to capture concepts and sound bites that cover the full range of points that you need touch on in a "stream of consciousness" manner. Reiterate this process in short spurts, take a break, then go at it again and again for a few days, until you feel you have gone dry with new ideas. During this first stage, there are no bad ideas or concepts as long as they are somewhat related to the key points that were identified earlier.

Focus especially on the call to action section, since this is the area where the rubber meets the road and where you will either get a nod for a desired next step—or get a turndown. Most elevator pitches do not have this section, so you'll have a leg up when you do. Write out at least five to ten action statements that you wish the listener to possibly take. These statements or questions need to spur desired actions associated with your goal—and be tailored to what your listener is realistically capable of doing to advance your fundraising process. If they are not likely to be a direct investor, asking them to do so is a waste of time and a lost opportunity. Even if they do not invest in firms such as yours, they may be a source of referrals to other investors or key employees, advisors, service providers, and so forth. Try not to waste an elevator pitch by closing with an inappropriate call to action.

The goal is to get at many ideas as possible down on paper. It is OK to return back to this first draft over several days and keep adding to it until you feel that you have reached a point where you have thoroughly covered each area in as many ways as you feel comfortable. You will know when you are done.

Then let it sit for a few days and come back to what you've written with fresh eyes and ears. Highlight the best portions and begin to whittle it down to a first complete draft. Once this is done, record it and listen to it objectively. It is important to listen to rather than read your draft pitch, since the spoken form will reveal additional information needed to fashion it into a final pitch. Listen to how fast you are speaking, where you emphasize points (or not) with your voice, whether you are using words that sound natural or not, and so forth. Refine the words and how you verbally present them, including where to modulate your voice. In addition, you need to do the following:

Practice. Try out your early versions on friends, co-workers, and advisors. Ask for their candid feedback and tell them not to worry about being polite. You are seeking brutal honesty at this point.

Memorize and tune. Commit your final version to memory so that you can easily and naturally repeat it in a conversational manner. As you begin to get comfortable with a final draft, add gestures and eye contact, and then make a video of yourself. Tune your body movements to appropriately reinforce the key pitch points. Double-check the final version of the video to make sure that you are within the 60-second time limit and that your pace of presentation is right.

Continue to improve. No matter how good you may think your first pitch is, expect to change it over time, based on interactions with investors. You may also need to develop minor variations to better match your audience. For example, if you are pitching to an engineer, you will want to emphasize the technology aspects.

Because elevator pitches are relatively short, many entrepreneurs do not invest the time to cover all the bases and try to "wing it." Now that you have better insights on not only what should be included in your elevator pitch, but also how to properly go about developing both long- and short-form versions, you are well on your way to landing many more investor meetings.

Good luck—and let's move forward!

ELEVATOR PITCH VS. TAGLINE

Do not confuse a tagline with an elevator pitch. I see it all too often in presentations. Taglines can be very useful in advertising materials, but they do not have a place when first attempting to gain the interest of an investor. The following are a few tagline examples.

- Cisco: We network networks.
- Brocade: Think fast. Think compatible. Think affordable.
- AT&T: Reach out and touch someone.
- GE: We bring good things to light.
- Acura: The road will never be the same.
- Harley-Davidson: American by birth. Rebel by choice.

Save the development of a tagline to later stages in your firm, when you have stabilized your business model and have a track record of growing revenues. Taglines are branding elements targeted primarily at customers—not investors.

Summary

Creating a successful elevator pitch to land investor interest is hard work, and it requires a minimum of particular data and information (our criteria) before it reaches a point of sufficiency. Reread the four examples and internalize what is good and bad about each presentation. Although the specifics of each example have been modified for the purpose of this book, I would like to note that whereas the first two examples did get funded by professional investors, the last two examples did not.

Start working on your investor pitch by mapping in your best answers/comments on all the identified criteria. Be objective and determine if you have sufficient content to reach at least an 8 out of 10 overall ranking against all eight criteria. Experience and background needs to be 10 out of 10—so if you have some minor weaknesses and want to overcome these concerns, find team members that beef up your corporate résumé. If necessary, don't be bashful about bringing in a more experienced CEO who can raise the probability of success.

Steps to Building a Successful Investor Presentation

Having developed and successfully used your elevator pitch to gain interest in next steps, you will need to prepare an appropriate slide presentation to go into greater depth about your firm.

Many people advise entrepreneurs to construct a business plan early in the business creation process. I agree with this viewpoint only to a limited extent because I have seen better business plans constructed *after* a good slide presentation has been first developed. As you will see in the following chapters, the development of a compelling investor slide presentation—using just 12 slides—will force you and your team to think through most of the issues that matter most to investors. Unless you can successfully tackle all of these basic issues and attract investor interest in next steps, including the start of serious due diligence on your firm, it is not likely that you will be able to successfully raise money, regardless of whether you have a business plan or not.

I have been fortunate to meet hundreds of entrepreneurs, as well as start many business ventures of my own. I see more of a "ready, fire, aim" approach taken by successful entrepreneurs who approach business development as a series of steps, starting with having an idea and creating an elevator pitch, then a slide deck, followed by a full business plan and detailed financials. The business plan and financials are mostly completed after investor interest has first been validated. Precious time can be wasted putting too much effort into a lengthy business plan and detailed financials, which nobody will care to read unless they first buy in to the fundamentals of your business idea—as presented in a tight slide presentation.

Tip Contrary to conventional wisdom, it's often better *not* to create an elaborate business plan and extensive pro forma financials until after you have created your fundraising presentation and elicited solid investor interest. Your emphasis—perhaps even your basic idea for the business—may well change after looking at a project through investors' eyes.

So, at the risk of alienating all the developers and fans of business plan software, my advice is to first focus on getting your basic business ideas out to investors for feedback, and save efforts for building detailed business plan materials until you have good validation. Of course, you will need to have basic financials developed in order to complete your slide deck, as well, so projections (as opposed to highly detailed financials, which can come later) are very important and must be done along with the slide deck.

As I have already written—and I will stress at least a few times going forward—the investment decision is highly a function of what investors think of you as CEO. They generally invest in the jockey, not the horse, and want to see you in action sooner rather than later. So if your elevator pitch has gained their interest, it is time to strut your stuff and give them a good show.

Why 12 Slides?

Without fail, most firms that we meet have far too many slides to build critical interest in the time permitted for typical first meetings. Large slide decks not only can keep you from getting critical feedback and buy-in from your investor audiences, but they also often—ironically—omit critical areas that investors need to understand in first meetings to want to move to the next step. Today's professional investors generally have a far more interactive style and want to share input and concerns—not be drowned out in an ocean of PowerPoint slides. Presentations that fail to cover the basic areas of investor interest, and that do not allow time for feedback and buy-in, are not likely to get you to second base.

As mentioned, fundraising requires that a series of hurdles are met before a check is written. Starting with a successful elevator pitch to gain attention and interest in a first meeting, your objective in the next meeting is to deliver a compelling investor presentation. Put another way,

The goal of this first meeting is to get the second meeting

And that second meeting will hopefully be the start of the more detailed due-diligence process that an investor will need to complete before writing the check. Your objective in the first meeting is to convince the investor to commit to next steps. You want to leave them with an "I'm interested—let me see more" attitude, rather than an "I don't get it—and I don't want to invest more time" attitude.

So again, why only 12 slides? Let's answer that question by first answering another question. In order to get a second meeting, what do you need to accomplish in this first meeting? You'll have the best chance of succeeding if you accomplish three objectives:

1. You validate your sector (i.e., there is a market for your solution).

2. You sell yourself as the person that can build and lead a team to the next level.

3. You convince the investor that your team can deliver a competitive solution to a large growing market that will—critically—*pay the right price*.

You are not there to get funded on the spot—or to present all the information investors will ultimately need to make an investment decision.

How Much Time Do You Have?

How much time do you have to make these three critical points? Typically, you will have one hour. However, in reality, you have much less time than that. Let's go through the math of a typical VC meeting:

*   5–10 minutes of icebreaking and introductions

*   20 minutes of Q&A

*   10 minutes for contingency

That means that, yes, you have just 20 to 25 minutes to make your three key points—and convincingly. So 20 to 25 minutes is what you should plan for! If you get more time, great; just don't plan your basic presentation for more time.

Also, if you are presenting at angel forums or fundraising conferences—which are even more time constrained due to multiple presentations that may be taking place—20 to 30 minutes, including some limited Q&A, is all you can count on.

Therefore, you should develop your core presentation around no more than 12 slides. Additional slides can be added to your deck as backup materials, but be prepared to achieve your objective of getting a second meeting by using no more than 12 slides.

Note   In most cases, you have less than a half hour to make your case to investors. The good news is that, if you prepare, that is enough time to reach the goal of the first meeting: to get another.

Summary

Fundraising is a process, not an objective. And you must successfully pass many hurdles before the money comes in. Like climbing a mountain, you need to start with the right preparation, and then take it one deliberate step after another until you attain your goal.

Up to now, you have learned how to target the right investors and give them a compelling introduction (your elevator pitch) to gain their interest. Importantly, you have gotten them to agree to a meeting (your call to action), and now it is time to present a succinct summary that hits on all the key points that they need to see and agree to in order to take further steps.

In each of the steps presented thus far, less is generally better and the same is especially true in developing your slide deck. This area is one of the hardest to apply the "less is better" approach. But once you learn the techniques ahead, they will stay with you for the rest of your career. It will also significantly sharpen your skills, so that you are ready when some young entrepreneur attempts to pitch you for investments as you become more successful.

Let's get on to the main event!

Title Slide and Introductions

Thanks to your persistence, you have secured a meeting with potential investors. The big day has arrived. You should be prepared with a professionally developed slide deck that you have memorized and rehearsed to the point that you do not need to refer to any notes. You should be so comfortable with the materials that—in a worst-case scenario—you could deliver an adequate presentation with no slides whatsoever.

There's one other thing that you should have done days, or even weeks, in advance. Again, it is critical that you do your homework before you arrive, and thoroughly know the backgrounds of those investors you will be addressing. There will be chitchat before the presentation begins, but believe me, it won't be idle. Professional investors will be sizing you up the minute you walk into the room.

Tip Have plan B at the ready. I always bring a backup slide presentation to meetings, either as a spiral-bound hard copy or on my iPad. Don't get thrown off balance by an impromptu change of venue, where you may end up presenting across a cup of coffee—far from any overhead projector.

Arrive at least ten minutes in advance in order to acclimate to the surroundings and get in a comfort zone. Get some water and engage in small talk with the receptionist if you feel that you need to shake off nerves and reduce your blood pressure before the meeting. You need to strive to attain a cool, calm, and confident CEO demeanor as a first impression.

Once you are ushered into the office or meeting room and have shaken hands with the investors, take a few deep breaths. When you are invited to begin, introduce yourself and any team members that are present with you. You should keep your team attendees to a minimum, because the investor or investors will primarily focus on you. Team members who can add value might include the firm's chief financial officer (CFO) or the vice president of engineering, especially if you believe the questions may go deeper into finances or technology than what you are comfortable answering. It is generally not a good idea to bring along other executives merely as observers.

Initial mutual introductions should take place in 60 seconds or less. Save team details, including your own detailed background, for later. It is good to mention appropriate common links or credible referral sources between you and the investors in order to help break the ice and get everyone loosened up. However, avoid throwing out names just to impress investors with the number of people you know. That can backfire. One or two common contacts is all you need (and make sure that they are good, deep contacts—not just someone you had a glass of wine with at last week's meet-up).

The First Two Minutes

Project the first slide (see Figure 7-1) right after your icebreaker comments, since you want the investor to become comfortable with you without the distraction of a bright slide on the screen.

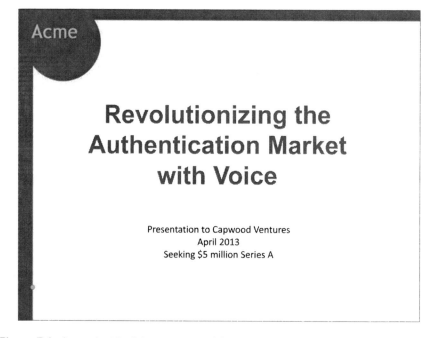

Figure 7-1. A sample title slide to present while you are building rapport, but before your actual presentation begins

You have two major objectives during the opening minutes before you flash the title slide:

- Build rapport
- Understand your audience

I've discussed the importance of building rapport right off the bat. Talk about people and places you have in common—schools, other investors or prominent business people, growing up in the same state, or what have you. The homework you did before you arrived will again prove invaluable; it will provide you with something to better connect you to the people who may become investors in your business.

As for understanding your audience, it's possible that you'll be thrown a curve ball. It is not unusual, for example, to be introduced to new people that you were not expecting to meet. It could be another potential investor, or it might be someone like a junior partner or the firm's Entrepreneur in Residence (many venture capital firms have an EIR). Often, junior people that join the investor are golden guys/gals-in-waiting, and they are the ones that perform most of the due diligence on your deal. If they are at the meeting, take that as a good sign, since investors do not bring colleagues to deals they don't like. Take the time to memorize their names (it's best to write them down—stress has a way of messing with your memory) and obtain brief information on their background. Try to understand why they were asked to participate and what their role might be going forward. This will help you with including them in your interactions, as well as with appropriately tailoring your remarks and questions.

After a minute or so of introductions, the investor's body language will tell you when they are ready to look at your presentation. Generally, the more time they spend engaged with you before the show starts, the better. Don't rush.

Some investors will quickly engage you with rapid-fire questions, even before you get started. Stay in control of the presentation and politely indicate that you will cover those points as you go forward. You should also state that you will present a *brief* overview of your firm by presenting *a few* slides, and that you will allow adequate time for a Q&A.

Tip Politely but firmly stay on track as much as possible, and do not quickly react to questions or get on tangents that won't allow you to get to key points in the available time. On the other hand, don't lose or frustrate your audience. If an issue cannot be deferred, address it and get back on track.

Convey the Right Attitude from the Start

It is very important that you guard against projecting an arrogant or know-it-all attitude. Otherwise, you will come across like bad cologne and kill your presentation before it gets started. A more humble "thanks for agreeing to meet with me and giving me an opportunity to present my company" attitude will put you in the best frame of mind. The following are some tips on what investors expect that a CEO do during a meeting just prior to starting our presentation. These will assist you with developing the right attitude and lead to a strong first impression:

- Listen more than talk
- Convey that you are open and respectful of input, and that you look forward to their advice and input during the presentation
- Thank them for the opportunity to meet
- Stay calm, smile, and maintain sincere eye contact
- Maintain good posture and project a "CEO aura"

It's a good idea to ask close colleagues and advisors about how you come across. It is often hard to make an objective self-assessment on how you project to investors.

Tell a Story

The first seconds of rapport building with prospective investors can be bumpy, and you need to allow a proper cadence to settle in for people to really begin listening to you. If you sense a communication-style disconnect developing, be prepared with some humor and/or a good opening story to warm up the room.

One of the best practices for a good start is to begin with a good story. This can start as soon as your introduction is done, when the investor signals that he/she is ready for the main event, and the first slide goes up.

Storytelling can be a powerful tool to get immediate attention and to set the stage for your presentation. The objective is to clarify what you do that customers care about and to connect with the people in the room. Great leaders are usually good storytellers, so consider it an opportunity to show your stuff.

Here are the ingredients for telling a good story:

- Keep it to about two minutes long.
- Hook 'em from the start so that they are now really anxious to hear the details that you are about to present.

- Make it compelling and memorable (something that they might share with their spouses at dinner later that day).

- Tie the story to your overall message.

- If possible, discuss potential customers who are experiencing pain in the absence of your solution.

- Consider telling what led you to the epiphany that caused you to start your business.

- Practice!

Note   Don't ever say anything about how you "couldn't keep a regular job" or that you've "always wanted to be a CEO." Saying such things to professionals marks you as an amateur.

The following are a few examples of good openers.

PI Diamond

PI Diamond, a company that makes low-cost diamond film used as heat spreaders on microprocessors, was seeking a Series B round of financing to expand their manufacturing capabilities. The CEO opened meetings with a literal icebreaker that was very successful in warming up prospective investors.

After introductions were made, he passed around thin diamond wafers to investors while his secretary brought in a fancy ice bucket filled with large ice cubes. He then asked each investor to pick up an ice cube and attempt to cut it with the edge of the diamond wafer. It turns out that diamond is such a strong conductor of heat, that the body heat generated by fingers quickly transferred across the wafer to its cutting edge, causing it to cut through an ice cube faster than a hot knife through butter.

This simple-but-compelling demonstration immediately set the stage for the CEO to talk about how his products dramatically improved microprocessor performance by reducing their operating temperatures.

Years later, I met investors who saw this deal (not all of whom invested), and they still remembered the company due to the clever—and literal—"icebreaker" by the CEO. "Yeah, those were the guys who could cut ice with diamonds . . ."

netDialog

In the mid-1990s, I was an officer in a software company that made a web-based product support system that allowed users to find quick solutions to frequently asked questions. This was before the days of web sites like Google and YouTube. We started every investor meeting by telling the story of how the company idea was developed when the founders, who were neighbors, attempted to put together a bicycle for one of their daughters on Christmas Eve. The manual was missing from the shipping box and they could not figure out how to put on the kickstand. In the process of trying to install it, they ended up badly scratching the paint on the bike, which got a very negative reaction on Christmas morning. Ultimately, they had to replace the bike to satisfy the daughter. In our opener, we described how our product would have solved this problem—even on Christmas Eve, when no one was staffing the help desk.

You had to be there to get the full impact of this story as an effective icebreaker—and younger readers might not fully understand what a big deal this was at the time—but we raised $10 million using this story as an opener for all of our VC and early customer presentations.

MicroTec Research

The founders were a couple of nerdy but likeable engineers who got the idea for the company by moonlighting as consultants. The CEO, Dan, often started fundraising presentations by talking about how these two partners used an early prototype that allowed them to debug new software very efficiently, and then charge so much money for their services that they could take vacations to exotic locations after each assignment was completed. The large fees that they earned confirmed that they created something that would dramatically increase the efficiency of creating new software—and encouraged them to start a real company, which we eventually took public and then sold to a larger public firm (a very nice two-bagger deal!).

None of you were born CEOs, and at one point in your careers, you probably thought that being a CEO might be an uncomfortable job. The same is true with storytelling skills. The process may not feel natural to you, but make it an objective and work on developing your own icebreaker story. If you find storytelling to be totally uncomfortable, work on other icebreakers to warm up the discussion:

- A provocative but pertinent fact that gains attention
- A relevant personal trait (curiosity, persistence, etc.)
- A quote from a famous person
- An appropriate joke (but be careful here—if you're not a person who tells jokes often, this could be risky at a moment you don't need to be)

Move on to the First Slide

It's important to understand the difference between a strong opening and irrelevant chitchat. There is a fine line here that you should avoid crossing, but you'll know where it lies when you start to stray from the opening remarks you have prepared. Resist the urge to do this. And be sure to get feedback from your colleagues on your warm-up approach in advance of your first real investor meetings. Try out more than one approach before settling on the one that best suits your personality.

Let's close this section by reviewing the content of the title slide. It should include the following:

- The name of your firm
- The date
- The name of the investor firm to which you are presenting
- Appropriate graphics (a logo, etc.) preferably against a light background that can copy well
- An indication of the amount of money you are seeking, as well as the investment round (e.g., Seed, Series A, etc.)

Note   Many CEOs delay presenting the monetary amount sought until later in their slide deck. In my experience, this is a mistake because most investors are generally quite narrowly focused when it comes to the amount of money and at what stage they care to invest. If you do not communicate this information on the title slide, you will risk losing the attention of your investor.

With the ice broken and a good connection made with your audience, it's time to click to the next slide.

Slide 1: Overview

You've made a connection with your investor, noted anything out of the ordinary (such as someone you didn't expect to be at the meeting), and told a good story. You have their attention.

In this stage of the presentation, you'll need to hook them with the strongest points proving that yours is an interesting investment. To develop the most effective opening slide (see Figures 8-1 and 8-2), put yourself in the investors' shoes and consider what they want to hear. As they watch your slide, you want them to be thinking things like:

- "This is a big market, crying out for a solution ..."
- "They appear to have something new that others do not have ..."
- "Real customers are seeing value in what they have ..."
- "I get it ... tell me more ..."
- "This might be the next big thing ..."
- "This guy knows what he is talking about ..."

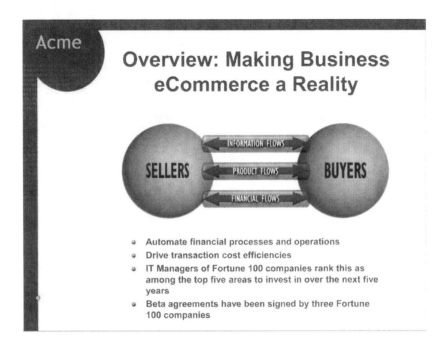

Figure 8-1. Overview slide that captures the problem and the solution, and provides validation

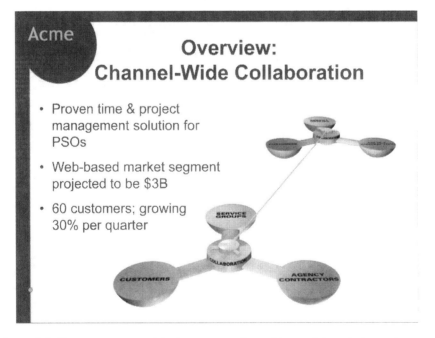

Figure 8-2. Variation overview slide that captures the problem and the solution, and provides validation

Once this attitude settles in, go back to your elevator pitch. Consider developing a graphic or perhaps using a photo that captures an image that reinforces your main theme.

We have found that slides that are heavy on images and light on text work best in these settings since investors will tend to listen and focus more on you if the key points come verbally from you. You need to presume that others who are not in the room will see the slides, so written words need to be included. Just keep them to a minimum so that you can verbally connect the dots and keep attention focused on you.

Using your best elevator pitch as an outline, Slide I should present an overview of your firm using two to five well-chosen, high-level bullets. They absolutely must grab investor attention.

Focus on the following:

- Getting immediate attention with your strongest assets (customer traction, investors, your team, etc.)

- Setting the tone for the rest of the presentation

- Briefly highlighting the 2–5 points that put your best foot forward; you will elaborate on those key points later

If you don't get their attention here, you won't get their check later.

Note   You have already written part of the script for your presentation of Slide 1—your elevator pitch. You've proven it works—it got you this meeting, after all—so give it again with as much (controlled) enthusiasm as you can muster.

When you first show this slide, deliver your full 60-second elevator pitch. Then speak to the points highlighted on the slide. The following lists the strongest points to include on this slide:

- What you do (using ten words or less)

- The size of the segment that your solution is addressing

- Traction: the number of customers, recent sales growth, the state of product development, and so forth

- Validation: a quote from a credible customer or a credible industry specialist, for example

- That you have assembled a superstar team that has previously made a lot of money for investors

Do not literally read the bullets. Instead, talk about them in an interesting manner. For example, the following might be a narrative that would accompany the first example slide (Figure 8-1):

> Our company is focused on dramatically lowering financial transaction costs between business buyers and sellers.
>
> Our specific focus area has been ranked by Fortune 100 IT managers in a recent IDG survey to be among the top five areas that they will be making investments in over the next five years.
>
> We have validated interest in our products from three Fortune 100 companies, which have signed conditional purchase agreements with us that represent potential sales in excess of $5 million per year for our firm.

For the second example slide (Figure 8-2), the entrepreneur could use a slightly different approach. After a short elevator introduction, he could immediately begin discussing how one well-known customer is using the product.

> Our company assists larger enterprise firms with utilizing their client services 24/7, simultaneously across multiple projects and time zones, thereby boosting their productivity and improving their bottom line by 50% or more.
>
> Our largest customer, [a global bank], is currently connecting client managers in their London and New York offices to provide seamless financial services support 24/7—resulting in increased revenues of 62%, without any increase in personnel.
>
> News of these productivity improvements is quickly spreading because competition between these firms is fierce, and we are benefitting from rapidly growing sales averaging 30% quarter to quarter.
>
> Our success is also allowing us to attract highly talented individuals from top technical schools across the United States, and enabling us to continue to expand our competitive edge.

Note also that these example slides do not overpower the presentation. It's better to use toned-down graphics—and deliver the punch that you need from the words that you say. Overly flashy slides cannot cover for a weak presentation.

As shown in the commentary in both slides, make your points quantitative rather than qualitative, if possible. In other words, present specific numbers rather generalities. If you have three customers, say that you have three customers—not that you have "some" customers. Investors are numbers people and generally react negatively to claims that are not precise or that come off as "warm and fuzzy." They won't, for example, respond well if you say, "We already have a number of satisfied customers."

Over 50% of the impression that you create with investors will be completed in the opening minutes and in the first couple of slides, so these first speaking points need to be as good as you can make them. Don't forget to use appropriate body gestures, make direct (but natural) eye contact, and take command of the room as you begin. It goes without saying, but practice until you know your presentation cold. Even script your hand gestures if you need to, but only if you can make them seem natural as you deliver them.

What to Expect

You will often know how well you are doing by carefully watching the reaction of the investors. So make sure you focus on them and not on your slide. If they begin to lean forward and appear to be drawn into to your comments, you will know you are heading in the right direction.

On the other hand, many professional investors are good poker players and will remain unfazed and not show any expression. Ironically, this can be a good sign because the absence of negative reaction is also a reflection of a desire to hear more.

If you start to pick up flak ("I don't get it." ..."Why are you any different?" ... "I don't agree with that.") while on your first slide, let the investor first fully vent his/her concerns before you speak. Your responses to objections and issues should start with acknowledging at least some legitimacy to the issues that are raised. But then follow up with additional information that gets the pitch back on track: "I agree with you. However, we discovered that large customers actually prefer our approach over those of competitors due to ...."

Tip Try to answer objections and doubts with references to customer feedback. It will be much more difficult for investors to challenge feedback from real customers. Also, avoid getting in a battle of opinions because that is a fight you will quickly lose. In any case, unsupported personal opinions do not carry much weight and can sink your chances.

You are almost ready to click to the next slide. But don't rush into the next slide until you are sure the investor has absorbed and accepted your comments.

Pause briefly, and then move on.

Slide 2: The Problem

Once you sense that your investors are OK with Slide 1 and that they remain interested, it is time to move on and discuss the problem that you are solving.

Early on in developing The 12 Magic Slides, my partners and I had a number of spirited discussions with investors and entrepreneurs about the pros and cons of emphasizing either *the benefits* that your solution provides or the *pain points/problems* that you solve. We discovered that, by far, investors are more interested in hearing you talk about solving problems! We also found that you can often describe the same product attribute either as a benefit to be enjoyed—or a pain to be avoided.

So in developing Slide 2, think about the compelling problem(s) that you are tackling. This slide (see the example shown in Figure 9-1) should describe "pain points" that your target customers feel and that your product will solve for them. But don't jump to the solution yet—stay with the problem and make them feel the pain.

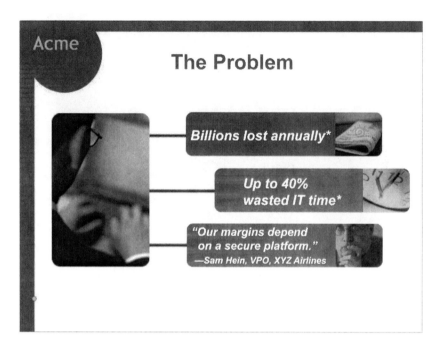

Figure 9-1. The Problem slide. Plan to describe the problem in detail without yet going into the solution

If you are targeting business customers, the pains points that you need to consider generally fall into the following categories:

- Revenue enhancement
- Cost reduction
- Faster time to market
- Market reach

There are many related and fundable problems that ultimately boil down and fit into these main categories. As an example, security enhancements may both lower costs and increase revenues. Faster computers may impact revenues and time to market, and so on. In very general terms, solutions that solve problems related to increasing revenues capture stronger investor interest.

As you move further from revenue enhancement, however, investors will demand more validation. Time-to-market and market-reach problems, for example, require much more substantiating data than revenue or cost-related problems. Not to say that other problems are not fundable—just be as objective as you can about your solution and position it as solving the most serious problem that companies face.

▓ **Tip** Everyone understands the need for more revenue and decreased costs. If your product solves those problems, good for you. But if your solution is about something other than those two items, plan to have substantiation that the pain point is valid.

Consumer Products Are Different

Consumer products have a similar hierarchy but even more categories, because emotions and perceptions play a larger role in influencing buying decisions. Consumers have a less rational side than business buyers and will often buy many products that solve more subjective problems, such as:

- Increasing their attractiveness to others with cosmetics or clothes

- Developing new skills, like learning a foreign language or a new sport

- Personal enjoyment in the form of a new speaker system or a music file download service

- Enhancing personal image, such as with a Rolex watch or designer blue jeans

- Improving health and well-being through vitamins or exercise equipment

The number of problems to be solved for consumers is endless and always changing. Ten years ago, did anybody really care about increasing the number of online friends they have? Then came Facebook. Or sending very short messages to others using a specialized application? Then came Twitter.

Broad generality alert: B2B (business-to-business) opportunities are easier to fund than B2C (business-to-consumer). Investors view the risk of solving bread-and-butter problems that businesses face, such as revenue enhancement or cost reduction, to be lower than betting on whether a new consumer item will be a home run. Facebook, Twitter, and countless other successful companies are exceptions, so I do not want to discourage you. I'm just pointing out that the bar is higher with consumer products—and so you should plan to work even harder to get a check.

Nail That Slide by Solving Serious Problems

You really have to nail Slide 2. To do so, have your team meet and develop a consolidated answer to the question: "What are the most serious problems we solve?"

- For our customers
- For our customer's customers (if B2B)

Select your problem area carefully. It has to be something your target buyer experiences regularly and that you know your product can alleviate. And be careful: do not confuse problems with solutions. For example, "faster," "better," and "smaller" are solutions, not problems.

For example, let's say that you have a start-up medical diagnostic device company that is solving the problem of detecting early-stage diabetes. The problem that you are solving is the detection of a disease that affects millions of people (big opportunity). Your solution offers faster, more accurate, and earlier detection than any other competitive product.

Let's take another example. What about a new hair-coloring product that you just invented? The problem that you are solving is to reduce the time and mess associated with current treatments. Your solution provides a superior result via a new shampoo product that works in less than three minutes (faster, better). Got it?

Validate the Problem with Quotes

It is best to include quotes from customers, which validates the existence of the problem. Quotes from credible industry specialists are weaker, but better than nothing. Ideally, quotes should contain the following:

- **We are experiencing (this problem):** "We are spending over $50 million per year on IT services solely focused on protecting our data from hackers."

- **This is a big problem that is not only impacting us, but many others in our industry:** "This is a major problem for financial services companies like us and it is getting worse."

- **We urgently need a solution, and after evaluating other options, we have selected [this company] to provide it to us:** "We have an urgent need to address this problem and have decided to go with [your company] after evaluating all other solutions."

You can also cite experiences with well-known customers who have directly confirmed the need for a solution like yours: "I recently met with a director of IT at General Motors in Detroit, who shared the story of a colleague who was fired due to the loss of data in one of their divisions. The GM IT director has committed to install our product right after the end of the quarter, and to give us a full-price purchase order if we can maintain his data integrity during a 30-day trial, which we are very confident we can do."

It is understandably difficult for most young companies to obtain such powerful quotes, but it must be a major objective to put in front of your sales and marketing team. You must demand that they cultivate customers or target customers to provide quotes/references that fit your overall message. Why is this so important? Customer quotes and references are among *the most important* criteria that determine if you get funded. And investors far prefer to hear quotes from real customers than opinions from very smart and persuasive entrepreneurs.

Note   Quotes from analysts or industry experts are best used to validate the size of the market, but not your product. If at all possible, you want a customer that has purchased and used your product to sing its praises.

What to Expect

By this point in your presentation, the investor is well along in sizing you up. If they are generally agreeing with your assessment of customer problems, they may not be saying much yet. If so, close this slide by asking, "Do you agree that we have identified an important problem that needs to be solved?" or "Are you interested in investing in solutions to this problem?"

If they are talking a lot as you present Slide 2, they are likely to be disagreeing with you. If so, hear them out, nod your head, indicate that you agree with at least some of what they say, and then offer up a "However, we discovered that…" and continue with customer feedback that reinforces your perspective (if you have it). If you are stumped, and they have really identified a hole in your assumptions, all is not lost. Ask them to share their perspectives, listen, acknowledge their views, and seek advice.

Most investors will not schedule a meeting to consider an investment unless they have general interest in your area. If they really don't like what you are doing, they will not take the meeting. So if you run into objections (at any point), take the time to understand their point of view and uncover the facts that they are considering that may be at odds with your data.

▦ **Tip**   As hard as it might be to ask, one question could be worth a lot of money to you in the long term: "Do you agree that we have identified a problem that needs to be solved?" You are talking to people who are experts in your industry, after all. Their insights can be worth a fortune, even if they don't invest in your project.

As you continue to move through the presentation, look for opportunities to obtain feedback from the investor and try to maintain a level of interaction. Watch them closely and you will see if they are staying with you, losing interest, or disagreeing. If you feel you have hit a speed bump, stop and ask a question. Better to take two steps back and regroup than to zip through the rest of your presentation.

Also, don't worry too much about the time. If you do, you will have a tendency to rush and not pay attention to important cues that might indicate that you are getting off course. Most investors will allocate about an hour for your presentation. If you are well prepared, you should be able to deliver The 12 Magic Slides in about 20 minutes. So go slow, ask questions, and keep the investor engaged—even at the risk of receiving some negative feedback.

Slide 3: The Solution

The Solution slide gives you the opportunity to explain your specific solution to the problem identified in Slide 2, *and* to explain and describe your overall business. Done well, you can accomplish both goals at once. In some cases, especially for start-ups, your solution is a description of the business.

In this part of the presentation, focus on the compelling customer benefits that you provide, with emphasis on the "must-haves"—not the "nice-to-haves."

The must-haves include tangible solutions that customers are willing to pay for; the following are a few examples:

- Lower blood cholesterol
- A faster Internet connection
- Reduced exposure to computer viruses
- A conference phone with superior sound quality

Nice-to-haves are ancillary features that, by themselves, will not compel a person to make a buying decision; examples might include:

- Extra USB ports on a new computer
- Rarely used applications on a new smart TV
- A generic address book–importing feature in a new social media application
- Rarely used key functions on a new wireless keyboard

Features can be very important—in fact, critical to certain buying decisions, especially when your major features are equal to other competitive offerings. However, your goal here is to settle on the top two or three reasons that make customers want to buy your product. If you can maintain investor interest here, you will have ample time later to discuss additional product details.

A defining graphic on this slide is preferred to a long textual description, because it allows you to maintain control of the presentation. The more text you use, the more investors will tend to read the slide rather than listen to what you are saying. If your solution has several elements, consider using overlays in your graphic so that you can better direct the flow of discussion and questions.

■ **Tip** Make sure the benefits you offer are all of the must-have variety. The world is filled with nice-to-have products, services, and ideas. But the must-have solutions cause people to reach for their wallets in numbers high enough to build a business.

Note the graphic used in Figure 10-1. It is meant to show that your application creates a barrier that protects essential computer applications, yet integrates easily. This graphic is more effective than simply showing a picture of computer, because installed software is invisible, of course. Instead, the graphic is designed to evoke a sense of what your solution provides—and your verbal discussion along with the terse text summary does the rest of the required job.

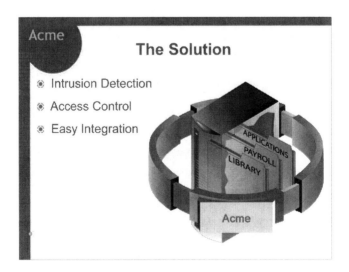

Figure 10-1. Simple-but-effective Solution slide

Keep in mind that simple professional slides work best and that you can easily overdo the graphics and lose control. This is not an art contest or designed to give your graphics designer a gold star. The slide is a palette to describe your solution.

Do not confuse the Solution slide with the Technology slide. That slide will come later. The Solution slide should show off features that provide tangible and very significant customer benefits. These benefits should differentiate you from your competition (else, what is the compelling reason an investor should buy in?) and that will cause your target customers to pay your price.

Before you give a presentation, develop several illustrations of your product or service and get feedback from your team, current investors, a mentor, or an expert to determine which representation works best to hook investors. You must find the right balance between a graphic that is simple enough not to distract attention from you, but at same time conveys the scope of your overall solution. This is a critical slide, and you should consider utilizing professional assistance so that the impression is very positive.

What to Expect

Anticipate that savvy investors who are focusing on your space have seen similar solutions before and will be looking for the unique and compelling differentiators that you provide. If you plan to charge a premium for your product, they will also look for reasons the strategy might work. Encourage good interaction on this slide to draw out the investor's initial thoughts on what you have presented so far. This is a good time to ask the following questions: "What are your thoughts on this?" and "How do you compare this with other solutions that you have seen?"

If an investor says, "I've sat through three presentations this month offering the same solution," don't panic. It can give you an opportunity to go into slightly more depth about your solution and to engage investors. But it's still better to preemptively acknowledge competitive solutions during your discussion points and volunteer your differentiators before questions are asked.

Here are some other tips:

- Investors look for big customer benefits in your solution. Make sure you emphasize your most compelling selling points.

- Customer validation is very important. Very few great products/services are developed without customer feedback. Talk about your interactions with credible customers. For example, you might say: "In our focus sessions with large target customers, they strongly felt that these features would make a significant positive impact on their business." Even better, if these customers said your products/services would reduce costs or raise revenues, and attached a figure, say so.

- Have a supply of customer quotes at hand to respond to skepticism about your solution. But don't adopt an "Oh yeah? Well, listen to what this customer said" attitude. Be respectful at all times; never become belligerent.

- Emphasize functional relationships, not technical details. Put another way: talk about the attributes that customers will pay for, rather than the technical details. For example, you should say: "This new cell phone only needs to be charged once a week," rather than, "We are using a lithium ion battery pack augmented with solar cells on the surface of the device." Save such details for the Technology slide (or as backup information).

- Define your "ecosystem," meaning other products and solutions that you interface with or impact, and show your relationship to and fit with adjacent solutions. For example, mention that your intrusion detection product easily integrates into all the latest IBM business computers.

Investors will signal that they are still with you at this stage by nodding their heads, leaning forward, and asking "tell me more" types of questions. On the other hand, if investors fold their arms, slump in their chairs, (or worse yet) start looking at their watches or smartphones, it is time to ask questions and restart their interest. Or find out what is not clicking and try to get them re-engaged. Your best fallback is to be well armed with customer anecdotes and testimonials. It is tougher for investors to argue against what customers say than what you might say.

Either way, solicit reactions from your audience to assure buy-in here. If you're not getting buy-in by now, you won't have another meeting.

Slide 4: Opportunity and Market

The Opportunity and Market slide gives you another chance to build your credibility with the investor as you share your analysis of the market opportunity for your product. Remember to match your market objectives to what your target investors typically are seeking. For example, technology investors (e.g., VCs) are looking for companies that address large market opportunities—typically $1 billion or more. Professional investors are also primarily focused on investing in firms that can attain revenues of $100 million or more within five years. Of course, you can expect them to be very skeptical of claims of a large market-size potential unless you can further qualify your ability to penetrate defined market segments successfully.

A common way to navigate this critical area is to use well-understood market segmentation terms along with an analysis of what your company is capable of attaining over the next five-year period.

TAM, SAM, and SOM

Classic market segmentation (see Figure 11-2) includes a discussion of the total available market (TAM), the served available market (SAM), and the anticipated share of market (SOM).

Total available market, also called the total addressable market, is a term that is typically used to reference the total market opportunity available in your target geographic region. For less mature US-based companies, the TAM is the United States, or possibly North America. For larger, more established companies that plan to market outside the United States, the TAM might include related international regions. The important thing to ask is, "How many businesses or individuals could buy a solution similar to my product or service?"

One approach to answering this question is to estimate the maximum market size that could theoretically be served with all competitive solutions, including your product or service. This could be stated in terms of customers, units sold, or (better yet) total potential revenues.

A subset of the TAM is the *served available market or SAM*. This is a segment of the total available market that you will target via your marketing efforts (given your focus and resources) over the next three to five years. Your anticipated *share of market or SOM* is the portion of the SAM that you actually plan to capture and derive revenue from in your business projections. For example, if you only have five employees (yourself and four others), what percentage of the SAM can you realistically reach in three to five years? The answer is the SOM.

Figure 11-1 shows projections of a TAM five years out, in 2018. The presenting firm is indicating that it expects to capture $100 million (its SOM) in that timeframe.

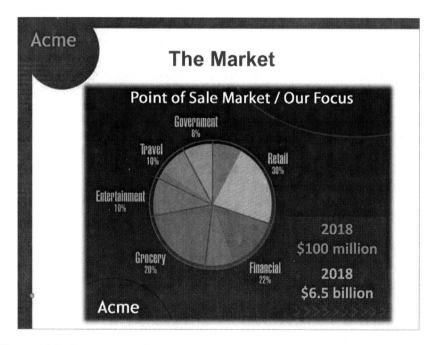

Figure 11-1. Simple market-focus slide showing anticipated sales of $100 million in a $6.5 billion market

It can be challenging and tricky to determine which TAM, SAM, and SOM figures you should use from among all the available market data. In order to withstand investor scrutiny, you need to think deeply about the figures that you use and their logical relationship to your business model.

▒ **Tip**   In this section of the presentation, as in all of them, keep your eyes open for intelligence that can turn your business around. One little insight—gained in a conversation with a potential customer, investor, supplier, or market expert—can turn around a business or provide the key needed to open the door to a big increase in sales.

Practical Examples of Segmenting the Market

Figure 11-2 provides the context for understanding TAM, SAM, and SOM. Let me now share some examples to clarify how these concepts can be used. We'll start with a simple example, and then go to a more complex one.

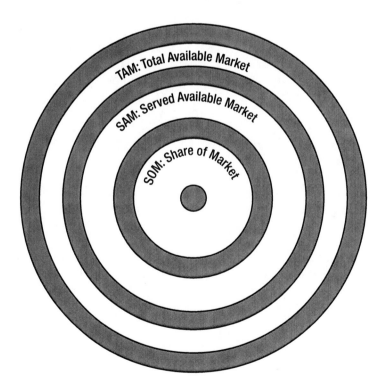

Figure 11-2. Relationship of TAM, SAM, and SOM

Ice Cream Business in New York City

TAM. Market studies indicate that the overall ice cream market in the United States is about $10 billion per year.[1] Although the firm is based in New York, New York, it is planning to expand across the United States within the next three years. So its TAM is $10 billion, which includes the sales of all competitors in its full potential market.

SAM. Remember, the served available market is the part of the total addressable market a company can reasonably expect to reach considering its business model. Although the actual percentage of ice cream sold in New York City is not reported in industry journals, an estimate of ice cream consumed can be made by considering that the population of New York City is equal to about 3% of the US population. Therefore, the SAM could be estimated to be 3% multiplied by $10 billion, or $300 million.

SOM. Recall that the share of market is the part of the SAM revenues that your firm reasonably expects to grab from the market, considering the practical limitations of the implementation of your business model. It often is a projection of expectations that can be reasonably achieved in three to five years. An ice cream company selling its products only in New York City cannot expect to sell all the ice cream sold in New York City. Assuming that it plans to sell only to supermarkets and restaurants, and that these channels represent 55% of all sales, and assuming that the company expects to achieve a 10% market share position, their SOM is $300 million multiplied by 55% multiplied by 10%, or $16.5 million in annual sales.

Medical Device Company That Diagnoses Vascular Disease

TAM. Research indicates that about 18 million people in the United States have a vascular disease, a potentially fatal condition that affects the circulatory system. About 10% of the entire population over the age of 60 has the condition—and the percentage increases as aging occurs. Only about 20% of these people have been diagnosed. Furthermore, like high blood pressure, patients are generally unaware that they have the disease because symptoms like dark spots on the legs, muscle pains, and so forth, are not generally apparent until the disease has progressed to advanced stages.

---

[1] International Dairy Foods Association, "Ice Cream Sales & Trends," http://www.idfa.org/news--views/media-kits/ice-cream/ice-cream-sales-and-trends/, 2012.

There are about 250,000 primary care physicians[2] in the United States, who (for the most part) do not perform any tests on their patients unless they receive complaints about possible symptoms.

The company has developed a device that allows primary care physicians to quickly and accurately diagnose the disease—even when obvious symptoms are not present. Each time a test is performed on a patient, US physicians are reimbursed by private insurance companies at about $125, regardless of whether the disease is detected or not, or by government health programs for fees as high as $3,600 per year for the life of a patient, if the disease is discovered. The device is rented (not sold) to physicians for $400 per month, regardless of the number of tests that are performed.

This example requires a bit more thinking about how to best calculate potential revenues and in sorting out relevant data from the facts that can be researched. After reflection, the data on the number of potential people who have vascular disease, as well as the percentage of those that are currently diagnosed, is not directly relevant in calculating the firm's TAM. Nor are the specific reimbursement dollars that physicians receive.

It is best to first ask: Who is buying my product?

Under the firm's chosen business plan, the paying customer for this product is the primary care physician. Obviously, physicians will not rent the product unless there are enough patients to warrant the investment (so the number of patients is important to know), *and* the physicians must also actually receive an acceptable amount of reimbursement. (The actual revenue comes from the doctors, of course.) Therefore, the annual TAM would be calculated as 250,000 multiplied by $400/month multiplied by 12, or $1.2 billion, in the US alone.

SAM. The firm has decided to focus only on primary care physicians who receive compensation under government healthcare programs in the US. These are the physicians that are likely to receive the largest reimbursements for each positive diagnosis. Presuming that about 30% of all primary care physicians fall into this category, the firm's SAM would be $1.2 billion multiplied by 30%, or $360 million.

SOM. The entrepreneur wishes to be conservative in setting investor expectations (a good practice!), and presumes that it will only be able to achieve a 10% market share within three years. Under these assumptions, its SOM would be $360 million multiplied by 10%, or $36 million in annual sales in Year 3 (after financing).

---

[2]A primary care physician is the general care or family practice physician that patients see first and most often before being referred to specialists, if needed.

Further Thoughts on the End Game: Size Matters

Now that you better understand basic TAM, SAM, and SOM concepts, you need to understand how investors will use your data to determine whether they should continue to invest more time looking at your business.

Ultimately, investors are most interested in how much money they can make from their investments. Your market share projections are primarily important to demonstrate that 1) you understand where you can win business, and 2) your market targets are large enough to produce acceptable returns given the size and risk of the investment.

However, the return on investment depends on something more than projected revenues and market share. Investors need to consider the future value of your business and what other investors will pay to invest in it either as a public company with traded stock or as an acquisition by another firm that will provide earlier investors with a liquid return and (hopefully) a higher value on their investment.

Investors will look at comparable firms in your sector and determine various value ratios that give at least an approximate sense of your future worth. One important thing that they will do (and that you should also do to be best prepared) is look at comparable multiples of similar public companies based on the ratio of their stock value to total revenues or earnings.

For the medical device company that I just discussed, industry comparables suggested a range of future value between 4X and 10X the annual sales. Using the lower end of this range, and the firm's projected SOM of $35 million, a future exit value of $120 million is possible—considerably more than the annual sales run rate.

The ice cream business, on the other hand, is in a business sector where traded comparables suggest a future value of only 1X to 2X the annual sales.

The other general way that investors consider the future value of their investment is to look at what another firm might pay to buy your firm. This approach requires some analysis of merger and acquisition transactions in your industry sector so that you can develop examples that can be shared with investors in the unlikely event that they do not have this data.[3]

---

[3]Merger and acquisition values for private firms can be obtained from attorneys, accountants, industry consultants, and, if the acquiring company is public, from public records that can be accessed via Edgar (www.sec.gov/edgar) or Internet sites such as Yahoo! Finance.

Most fundamentally, the value of a firm to another firm is largely based on your "accretive value." Basically, this means that your value approaches the full value that can be realized by the acquiring firm through leveraging all that you have developed. Accretive value (see Figure 11-3) can often result in very large returns for investors, and it is important for you to fully understand at least some plausible exit scenarios to discuss with investors.

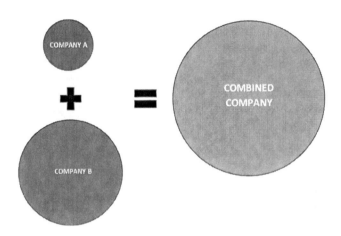

Figure 11-3. This example of accretive value shows that the value of the combined companies is greater than each separate firm

Accretive Value in Practice

Let's go back to our medical device company example to demonstrate how accretive value works.

One of the larger firms in its industry sector, a multibillion-dollar public firm, sells surgical equipment and products that treat vascular disease. The accretive value of our device company might be substantially higher to them than a public IPO valued at $120 million. As highlighted, only about 20% of vascular disease is currently diagnosed—and the large public firm currently enjoys a multibillion-dollar market value based on the sales of their products to treat these patients around the world.

If this device could substantially improve the diagnosis rate, the larger firm would likely gain many more new patients that would have a need for its products. A case could be made that the market value of the acquiring company would increase by significantly more than the $120 million market value projected for the device company if it were publicly traded.

In Silicon Valley, there are many examples of relatively small and young companies that get acquired for breathtaking sums of money that initially appear way out of reason. However, "accretive value" is often the justification for the purchase price.

What to Expect

At this point in the presentation, it should be increasingly apparent whether or not the investor is on board and liking what they have heard so far. Also, for better or worse, you have made your first impression and are now onto showing your deeper knowledge of the market opportunity. Seek feedback and buy-in, and search for any unanswered concerns that may be lingering issues for the investor. This is an important slide and you need to make sure you have buy-in before moving on.

You can ask a very good question to confirm that an investor is on the same page as you: "Do these market assumptions seem reasonable?" If the answer you receive is anything other than a solid yes, do not move on without probing further with follow-up questions such as: "What changes would you suggest?" or "Is there any follow-up data that I can provide?"

At this point in my firm's workshops, I sometimes get the following question:

"But Paul, I have only 20 minutes to give my pitch. Shouldn't I just move on and make sure I cover all my 12 slides rather than get bogged down on a couple of slides?" The answer is emphatically "No."

Your first and main objective is to establish your personal credibility with the investor. If you succeed, you will likely have a shot at a follow-up meeting where you can cover other details. If you miss picking up on a disconnect that develops during the presentation, you will not only not get a follow-up meeting, but you will likely wonder what went wrong and repeat the same mistake with other investors. It is far better to blow a presentation and get feedback on the spot, which can make you more effective on your next pitch, than to rush through your 12 slides and not understand why your follow-up calls and e-mails are not returned.

Even if you do not cover all 12 slides, the investor will have your slide deck and a pretty good idea of what else you planned to cover. Engagement and appropriate interaction trumps rushing through your slides. Still, you should strive to perfect your presentation to the point where you can deliver all 12 slides and still have an appropriate amount of interaction.

> **Note**   I am reminded of one of the most common questions that I receive from entrepreneurs: "What is the most important slide?" To that I typically respond, "This one." No matter what the slide. Truth is, they are all important. Otherwise, you would not be discussing them. And each slide presents unique challenges that you must overcome to successfully maintain investor interest in order to get to the next slide—much like Indiana Jones chasing the missing Sivalinga stone in *The Temple of Doom*.

As you can see from this discussion, the Opportunity and Market slide requires a fair amount of analysis and understanding—and unwary entrepreneurs (or even very experienced ones) can make serious errors in positioning the potential of their opportunity with investors.

I'll provide an example. My partners and I recently met with an enthusiastic CEO of a software company who shared his vision of how his firm was going to penetrate a large retail consumer market. It quickly became clear to us that the limited financial resources of the company would not accommodate execution of this large objective. Instead, we convinced him to refocus his marketing on larger established companies and sell his software to them on an OEM[4] basis so that they could utilize their larger economies of scale to penetrate the retail consumer market. While his sales projections were negatively impacted, his profitability went up significantly under this segmentation model, and most importantly, he had enough money to successfully execute the revised strategy, whereas his original strategy would have failed.

Companies also often shift market focus as they mature, and new market segments can open fresh opportunities that may even be larger than originally contemplated. The CEO of the medical device company revealed to me that three years after the company was formed, physicians began telling him that his marketing focus was "all wrong" and that he needed to focus on physician groups that were involved in managed-care programs. Acting on this unexpected insight significantly increased market penetration and hastened the timing of the firm's IPO.

Keep in mind that the investors watching your presentation will be thinking long term—especially to eventual exits. So do not complete this slide without first thoroughly understanding exit value scenarios for your firm. Then work backward on market segmentation analysis to validate and ensure that your projections are in line with investor expectations and can withstand scrutiny. Anticipate tough questions—and have answers for them.

Since most investments tend to exit via M&A than IPO, I'd encourage you to invest more time studying M&A economics and the principles beyond the very basic fundamentals presented in his section.

---

[4]OEM is an acronym for Original Equipment Manufacturer.

Slide 5: Technology

Slide 5 (see Figure 12-1) provides an overview of your technology and intellectual property (IP).

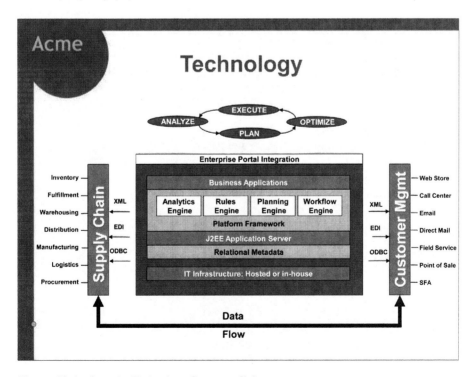

Figure 12-1. Complex Technology Overview Slide

But First: Will Investors Steal Your Ideas?

Before we cover the Technology slide, let me cover an important question: What should you do to protect your ideas from getting stolen by investors?

You may not like my answer, but if you want to maximize your funding chances, the answer is "Not very much."

Let me cover the basics and explain the way the real world works.

In spite of what many attorneys, well-wishing friends, and advisors may tell you, professional investors will rarely sign any confidentiality or non-disclosure agreements (NDAs) prior to seeing your pitch. Furthermore, if you lead with this type of request, many investors will take no further steps with you and write you off as being too naïve to be ready for their investment.

There are many reasons that investors give for not signing an NDA, but the following are key ones:

- It is impossible to keep track of NDAs when you are looking at a lot of deals. Even if you have an administrator keeping meticulous track of every NDA, it is very, very difficult to sort out new technologies and compare them to others that you have seen to determine if you are about to infringe on a previous agreement.

- The classic sentiment that "ideas are a dime a dozen—it is all about execution" is largely true. You may have the best method for packing more memory into a sliver of silicon, but if you can't do all the heavy lifting required to fully implement the idea, your idea is worth very little, if anything.

- Even if your key concepts are patented, there is a whole industry of intellectual property (IP) attorneys that make a good livelihood challenging patents and working on behalf of firms with larger financial resources to effectively find ways of utilizing (some would say "stealing") someone else's patented technology. Even a casual search of patent fights reveals that most are settled with some sort of royalty agreement that allows the offending party to continue to use the defendant's technology after agreeing to pay some damages and an ongoing royalty.

So, by sharing your technology, are you basically opening yourself to getting screwed and run over by a larger, better-financed competitor? Maybe, but that is the price to pay if you're seeking outside capital. Obviously, just about every entrepreneur that raises capital has confronted this issue. What did they do?

- Your best form of protection is to take steps to execute your ideas better than anyone else.[1]

- Stick with reputable investors who have a track record and whom you trust. I have made the point elsewhere in this book about picking your investors carefully, and that advice also applies here.

- In spite of my comments about patents, they are still very important and can provide protections. In addition, limit the exposure of your trade secrets and other "secret sauce" aspects of your technology (e.g., the famous and secret Coca-Cola formula).

Realize that the vast majority of investors are looking to make money by investing in good deals, not in pirating other people's ideas. The bottom line: forget about NDAs, take reasonable precautions, and don't open your kimono more than you need to to land your investor.

I will have more comments on this as we continue.

Present Your Technology

Now, on with the show. The technology section of your presentation is not a listing of patents, but rather a high-level summary of your "secret sauce" that is designed to satisfy technically rigorous investors. As with other slides, this is not meant to be an all-inclusive view of your full technology, but more of an overview to provoke Q&A that should lead investors to better understand what is technically unique about your solution.

There are many ways to approach this slide and I have not seen two that are alike (as you might expect). However, there are some best practices. First, strive to create a diagram that summarizes your major technology components by using terms that should be known to the investor. This can be tricky, since your engineering team will typically be using acronyms for many of the detailed components. You may need to use clearer labels and to describe important areas in layman's terms.

---

[1] As an extreme example, bottled water can sell for up to several dollars per bottle, yet the same amount of tap water can be obtained for free from a public drinking fountain. Firms such as Coca-Cola, PepsiCo, and Nestle derive hundreds of millions of dollars in profit by selling bottled water, a concept unheard of as recently as 30 years ago. This is an example of an execution play at its best!

Next, if you have several technical components, consider building a simple basic slide, and then add overlays to it that you can click through and highlight as you discuss your approach—component by component. Figure 12-1, for example, has several key elements that were introduced and discussed, one at a time, by the presenter. Unlike the other slides, which present more limited and focused information, the Technology slide is one in which you can get away with presenting more information, especially if you have a very technical product and you are addressing an engineering-type investor.

The second of the two example Technology slides (see Figure 12-2) is a more general "ecosystem" slide that shows only macro components and relationships with other technologies. This type of slide works best if

- Your solution is less technical.

- Your audience is less technical.

- Your products largely consist of existing technologies that you are integrating rather than developing from scratch.

- Your main company differentiators are in nontechnical areas (for example, you have a new sales or marketing approach).

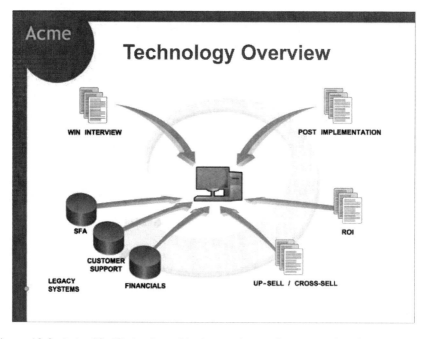

Figure 12-2. A simplified Technology slide that emphasizes functions rather than nitty-gritty details

Invent vs. Integrate

Among the areas that you must highlight are those in which you are inventing or developing something that provides differentiation. But make sure that the differentiation *is important to your customers and will favorably impact their buying decisions.* If you are an engineer, or if you are having your engineering team develop this slide, be wary of a tendency to include and emphasize items that need to be built but do not matter much to customers.

An example might help drive this home. One of the latest "cool" programming languages used to build sophisticated web sites is called Ruby. The related development framework is called Ruby on Rails (RoR). Without getting into all the technical nuances, many engineering-types tend to gush over web sites that have been built using this language. And if you build your site/application using RoR, your engineering team will likely want to pat themselves on the back and have you emphasize RoR (as opposed to just listing it) on your Technology slide. While some investors may see this as an interesting differentiator, it is far more important to emphasize the customer benefit that RoR might provide, like increased security or greater compatibility with more mobile devices relative to your competitors.

So while your diagram may include Ruby on Rails, your comments about it might be: "We built the applications using Ruby on Rails in order to provide a more secure environment that could be accessed by more mobile devices than our competitors. These areas are highly sought after by our target customers."

Tip When you talk about technology, don't talk about what it is so much as what it means for customers. Remember, your goal is to solve customer problems, not show off engineering feats.

Once you highlight the invented areas that interest customers, you should also discuss major third-party components of your solution that you are integrating or licensing, or otherwise using. As an example, if you are building a cloud-based application,[2] you might say, "In order to better meet the security and cost objectives sought by our target customers, we are hosting our application on Amazon's EC2[3] platform."

Investors want to better understand the balance between what you invent and what you plan to outsource or integrate from third parties so that they can be assured that their investment dollars are being focused more on

---

[2] A software application having certain components hosted on Internet servers at a remote location and that are typically leased from a third party.
[3] A popular application hosting service provided by Amazon.com.

building unique differentiators, and not so much on developing components that can be obtained from third parties.

Another area that you must highlight relates to the relationship of your solution to pertinent industry standards and platforms used by your target customers.

As an example, if your customers are primarily using Microsoft-based computers and Android smartphones, you will fall flat if your solution only runs on Apple-based products. Investors will also be very nervous if they hear that your approach includes creating new standards that compete with existing standards.

The issue of standards and platforms is a dry topic, so don't dwell on them excessively or on which specific standards you comply with. However, investors must feel that you are not about to waste their money or put their funds at greater risk by going off into some unchartered area. Use a simple statement, such as "Our solution is compliant with all industry standards used by our customers, and it is designed to simplify easy adoption."

As with other slides in this initial presentation, keep in mind that this is an overview slide. Volunteer to present a more complete technology summary and future road map during a follow-on meeting.

What to Expect

There are a number of landmines that you must avoid stepping on when presenting the Technology slide. Among them are the following:

- Your opening comments need to stress that you are providing a high-level overview, and that more information is available and can be shared in a follow-up meeting. If an investor wants to drill down deeper and starts to engage you in a technical back-and-forth exchange that goes longer than a minute or so, get back on track by stating, "That is a great question and one that our engineering team can address in a follow-up meeting with you."

- Avoid taking your VP of Engineering to a first investor meeting. If they insist on attending, coach them to remain on the sidelines and allow you to stay on track. If they get asked a question that can be answered quickly, such as "When do expect to complete the next release?"—no problem. However, if it gets much deeper—like "Why did you decide to program this application using Ruby rather than PHP?"—coach them to defer this type of Q & A to a later meeting.

- Keep the geek-speak to an absolute minimum while emphasizing the unique customer benefits that you are creating and that will drive sales. It is desirable and appropriate to express your personal knowledge of your technology, but strive to hit a least common denominator (i.e., speak as if you are talking to the least technical person in your audience) and do not use too many acronyms.

- As with other slides, close on this slide by obtaining feedback and acknowledgement that your investor buys in to your approach (or at least does not have any serious objections) and remains engaged and interested in moving on to your next slide. A good way to close would be to ask, "Does this seem like a reasonable approach to meeting customer requirements?" If you get any other answer than yes, stop and obtain feedback, and try to confirm interest in a follow-up meeting where you can better address concerns.

As we conclude this chapter, notice that the suggested discussion of your technology has been accomplished via a mostly high-level, building-block style where you avoided deep exposure of your proprietary intellectual property. Many entrepreneurs are nervous about presenting this slide and fearful that investors will either pick them apart or share details with another similar company that they prefer.

Strive to strike a balance between what you present and any genuine concerns about sharing too much. You do not need to "give away the store" to successfully discuss your technology at this initial step.

Slide 6: Unique Competitive Advantages

Slide 6, Unique Competitive Advantages (see Figure 13-1), is an important slide. Following the unique areas that you discussed in the Technology slide in the previous chapter, you now need to fill out the full scope of competitive advantages that you believe will help you win new customers and grow your business.

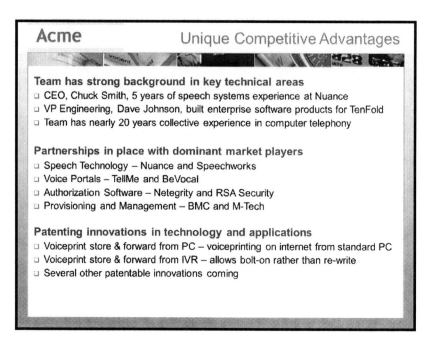

Figure 13-1. *Unique Competitive Advantages slide example*

It's All About People, IP, and Relationships

Your unique technical or proprietary advantages will likely fall into one or more of the following areas:

- People
- Intellectual property (e.g., patents, non-publicly disclosed "secret sauce," domain expertise, trademarks, brands, etc.)
- Business relationships that provide your firm with faster access to key market segments and customers

As you begin considering items to emphasize on this slide, ask yourself if each point helps to win you more customers or increases investor confidence that you will be more successful.

What you discuss on this slide should be those advantages that relate only to these areas. Let's go into more detail.

People

Generally speaking, I recommend that you begin your discussion of unique advantages by highlighting up to three key team members or overall team attributes that are most closely related to providing competitive advantages to your firm. You will have an opportunity to present your management team in more detail on Slide 10, The Team, so for now you are presenting only a high-level summary of the most potent team attributes that will positively impact your firm's ability to effectively compete. You might include the following team members:

- Key executives with deep industry backgrounds and whose prior experience and personal networks can accelerate achieving your objectives

- Senior technologists that have developed similar products successfully

- If you are later stage and have revenues, you might consider highlighting a sales/marketing executive who can rapidly build a team from his/her former team members[1]

You should not list all senior team members (again, save that for Slide 10) but instead only highlight your key executives with strong experience in accomplishing objectives similar to those tasked to their roles in your firm, and ideally, who have been notable contributors in prior firms that generated good investor returns.

Also, list those team members who are closely involved with what you plan to accomplish with the funds from the current investment round. If your deal is seed or early stage, you should emphasize technical people over sales and finance people—especially if your objectives relate to the technical execution of a first product. If you are later stage, highlight your sales and marketing executives, and if you nearing an exit event such as an IPO or acquisition, your CFO should be included on this slide.

Be forewarned that the selection of people for this slide can cause friction within the ranks. As a CEO, you don't want to look like you are playing favorites, so you need to explain in objective terms why only certain people will be named. Unless the choices are obvious and there are no expected residual personnel issues, plan to gather your executive team together when this slide is being created and state the following: "I'd like to get everyone's opinion

---

[1] Investors understand that recruiting top people is one of the greatest challenges that growing companies face. Therefore, it is a common practice to hire senior executives that can quickly recruit people who they have hired and worked with before. This is a very important attribute to seek when hiring senior team members, and the presence of such executives on your team can be important to highlight on this slide.

as to who will be the most valuable contributors in helping us pull off our planned objectives for this investment round." This approach might help you deal with a prima donna who might otherwise conclude that he is not being appreciated.

Intellectual Property

Presuming that you adequately covered your technology differentiators in the previous slide, summarize them in a one-liner here (it doesn't hurt to repeat), then add other nontechnical areas that comprise your "secret sauce." These areas can include trade secrets, novel marketing and sales approaches, a brand that you have acquired that gives you added market presence, and so forth.

Business Relationships

Focus on relationships that 1) help you better connect and land customers, 2) reduce costs, and 3) improve operating efficiencies. As examples, you might consider including exclusive distribution-and-marketing alliance partners, an outsourcing manufacturing or logistics firm, or a relationship with a highly effective search engine optimization (SEO) firm. Once again, select the relationships for this slide that best relate to the objectives that you plan to accomplish at this funding stage. If you are an early-stage firm and have a unique and strong relationship with an investment banking firm that might help take you public, save it for later—when that relationship will be important.

Investors are expecting you to make a strong case for why any stated barriers to competition will not be easily overcome by larger and more established firms who may choose to follow you. The most common defense against competition is "first mover advantage." Many entrepreneurs claim that they will beat the competition because they will be the first to exploit some newly discovered market advantage. While being first to market can be a powerful differentiator, investors will be skeptical of this claim unless you can provide solid validation in the form of sales, successful tests, customer praise, and so on. If you plan to make this assertion, be prepared to back it up.

Tip Investors hear the phrase "first mover advantage" often enough that it raises their skepticism. If you intend to use it, plan to provide proof that you will indeed be first to market with a large advantage. If your offering is similar to other solutions but better in performance, be sure to emphasize how much better in quantitative terms; for example: "We are ten times faster than [our next closest competitor]."

How to Present This Slide

As you begin this slide, start with a brief overview of your advantages. In particular, the following sentences can be powerful. Complete them based on your unique situation.

- "We are the first company to ..."
- "We are confident that our [product/service] will give us a significant lead over our competitors."
- "Top customers have evaluated us against competitors and prefer our solution because of ..."

Next, you'll want to emphasize the strength of your team and key individuals; Avoid a verbatim reading of the text on the slide and instead provide a verbal summary. For example: "Our engineering team consists of the most capable scientists and developers in this area, with prior experience in building similar successful solutions. Two of them worked for [Company X], which had an IPO last year that made its founders millionaires."

Unique domain expertise can also be important: "Our executive team has over 100 years of collective experience in developing CMOS-based technology solutions for networking chips."

Unique business relationships can be equally important. You might say, for example: "We are unique in having a relationship as a supplier to [Fortune 500 company] that will give us a significant edge in penetrating [our target market]."

Next, don't forget to provide any critical new advantages that you have over your competitors, especially those that have been validated by customers. For instance: "Our SEO partner has succeeded in getting us at the top of more than 50% of Google searches with key words that customers use to seek similar solutions. None of our competitors can claim this advantage." Or: "We are the first to discover how to utilize stem cells from pig embryos to create new organs that will not be rejected."

Finally, as you can imagine, intellectual property (patents and "secret sauce") can be powerful motivators for investors. If you can do something that no one else can—for the next 20 years—you might have license to print money. Tout that fact: "We have three patents filed, with two more pending, and we have a solid technology road map that extends out three years. These patents will give us performance advantages that no one will be able to match for several years."

A few words on patent-related discussions. As important as patents can be in establishing that you have created valuable IP, most investors do not put as much weight on patents as they do on execution. They also frequently prefer that their precious investment funds do not get overly allocated to funding expensive and time-consuming patent filings. It really depends on the segment. If yours is a drug company, patents are very important. In social media, less so.

However, in a first meeting, it is rare that investors will challenge patents or even have you discuss them in any detail beyond what I cited earlier. To the extent that there may be patent issues or questions, these types of issues are usually raised in subsequent meetings.

Alternate Slide Formats

The most common approach that we see for the Unique Competitive Advantages slide is the "snapshot" format shown in Figure 13-1. This slide allows you to address, without too much future speculation, the areas that I have previously outlined. But if your company is less mature in its development cycle and lacks perceived critical features, Figure 13-2 is also quite common as an alternative, and as opposed to the "snapshot" format of Figure 13-1, this variation shows the evolution of your feature set over time. I recommend that you also prepare a form of this slide as a backup slide, since it is common for investors to ask about future planned enhancements. You can either have that discussion at the first meeting, if it is brief and you have the time, or you can try to set up a follow-up meeting to cover this and any other questions that come up that cannot be easily answered in your first meeting.

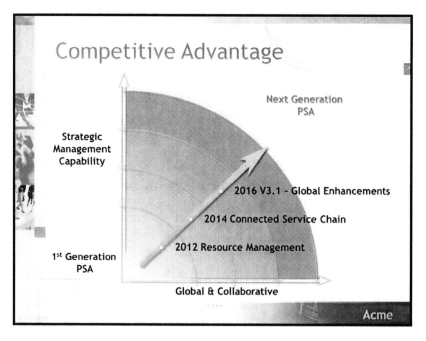

Figure 13-2. Alternate competitive advantage slide

One caution with this alternate slide: if too many critical features are "futures" and this slide creates an impression that you will not have a salable product until future funding rounds are completed, expect significant push back or even a hard no. Be clear about when you will have a salable product and emphasize future enhancement as a means of gaining further market share from your competitors.

Best Practices

As suggested with other slides, prepare the points you wish to make on this slide by first developing a laundry list of all possible competitive advantages. Share this list with your team and agree on weighting criteria that will allow you to rank-order your advantages. Emphasize the advantages that...

- Cause customers to buy your products over those of your competitors.

- Are most defensible for the long term.

- Will have the greatest positive impact on your revenues and profits.

On the other hand...

- *Avoid differentiators that are "gee-whiz" features possibly liked by your engineers, but that do not impact revenue growth.* This is one of the most common problems that weaken otherwise good presentations and cause investors to believe that you have a poor understanding of what matters most to your customers. Rigorously determine the value of each listed feature to your customers. If you cannot easily connect the dots, remove it from this initial presentation.

- *Avoid differentiators that are fleeting and easily duplicated by larger competitors.* As I am writing this section, Apple just announced the iPad Air. While many Apple zealots love this product, declaring it to be the best tablet of all time, more astute and objective customers are scratching their heads wondering what all the fuss is about. The product's chief new features are that it is lighter, thinner, and faster than the previous model. In a broadcast interview of people outside the flagship Apple store in New York, no one expressed interest in buying one except one six-year-old girl. Investors understand that such features are quickly eclipsed by competitors and do not lead to strategic differentiators that will result in high investor returns.

- *Avoid differentiators that are speculative and do not have significant validation from customers, and which give rise to the question, "Who cares?"* A listing of features without obvious customer benefits is one of the surest ways to kill interest from investors. Any hint of a "build it and they will come" attitude from you or your team, and you can be confident that you will not be successful with professional investors. When entrepreneurs were challenged with this type of input in our workshops, they were often quick to cite exceptions of new products that became megahits (e.g., the iPod) without any apparent customer validation. It is fair to say that those types of products exist. However, astute investors play the averages and place many more bets on validated products and features.

Tip   Avoid a "we will build it and they will come" attitude. You must present significant validation that customers have come or intend to.

Set the Follow-up Hook

A good guideline is to stick to your top three differentiators, covering no more than three general areas (with no more than nine differentiators in total) and save any others for follow-up discussions. At various points in your presentation, look for opportunities to set the hook for follow-up activities with your investor or their assistants. As stated many times, an overriding top objective for this first meeting is to create interest, and ideally, a commitment for a follow-up meeting. As you continue with your presentation, try to set more and more hooks for a subsequent meeting. But importantly, don't close on the meeting until you are completing your wrap-up.

You might set another hook for a follow-up as you conclude this slide by stating something like the following: "Customers have told us that they select us over our competitors due to the following three unique items... In addition to these key areas, we have several other desirable areas still in development, which will maintain our lead in this area. We can share those with you in a follow-up meeting, if you like."

The reaction to this type of question at this point in your presentation will tell you quite a bit about how you're doing. Any positive reaction, even a mild nodding of the head, for example, will be great feedback and increase the confidence with which you will deliver the remaining slides. If the investor is suggesting interest in a follow-up meeting at this stage, you are close to batting a thousand. Yet, hold back, stay in control, and wait for your final summary and call to action before setting the next date and time. If the investor is not yet biting, look for hooks as you present the remaining slides.

What to Expect

You can be sure that the following questions will be in the minds of astute investors listening to your pitch. So prepare good answers in advance.

Are these competitive advantages yours alone? Your best answer is to start with a customer anecdote along the lines of the following: "A vice president of purchasing at [Fortune 500 company] told us that he was waiting until this feature set is available before placing a substantial sales order—and we just received his first order." A less compelling—but still good—answer is to share market research reinforcing a market need that your solution uniquely provides. When the iPad was first announced, for example, there were many other tablets that had preceded it and none had met with any success. Unlike all the others, the iPad launched with hundreds of new, low-cost applications ready to go, and as a result, it rapidly and strategically outdistanced all its competitors. It continues to do so to this day.

Will the benefits provide a 10X+ advantage? Investors like companies that significantly move the needle. Small, incremental advantages do not get them excited. Make an effort to quantify the totality of the impact that your solution has on customers relative to your competitors. Many times this is hard to do, and you may also confront the harsh reality that what you plan to create may not be that great after all. If so, push yourself and your team to develop advantages that provide customers with BIG benefits. The overall impact does not actually need to be 10X, of course, but it *must* be very significant in order to allow you to get funded.[2]

How long will the advantages last? There are hundreds of new cell phones announced every year, each having relatively minor advances that are quickly eclipsed by competitors. While those types of fleeting advances sell more phones, they do not meet the needs of investors, who are often making bets that are not expected to provide an exit for ten years or longer. If investors think your advantages will hold for just six months or a year, they will not write a check. What they want to hear is that you have a couple years to roll out the product while staying out ahead of the pack, and that you have a long-term

---

[2]In almost every workshop that we conduct, we find companies with weak advantages over others in their market. We often ask the CEO and his team to do some deep soul-searching on how they can improve their overall position, and then extend an invitation to return to a future workshop. While many teams just leave, never to be heard from again, a surprising number come back with a new insight that reinvigorates their pitch and company direction. As the saying goes, "Think big and you might surprise yourself."

plan to stay ahead until a satisfactory exit has been attained. Your comments on this slide should provide at least one sentence of reassurance that you have a long term advantage: "Our access to the Chinese market, through our unique relationship with Alibaba, gives us at least a five-year jump on our competitors."

What will it take to overcome your advantages? Stress your "people" advantages if you sense this question to be an obstacle. Great team members (assuming you have them) cannot be replicated, and their presence on your team adds significant support to claims of your long-term sustainability. Frankly, for some firms, factors such as technology barriers, marketing and sales advantages, and so forth, are more easily overcome through "zingers from left field" that nobody sees coming. Great people do not provide surefire insurance against the impact of truly transformational changes, but their presence does cause investors to be more inclined to open their checkbooks.

Why will customers care? Always go to investor meetings armed with a number of customer anecdotes and testimonials. Even if you have no real paying customers, you must have feedback from potential customers ready to share as the need arises. Sprinkling customer feedback throughout your presentation is a powerful way to keep your investor interested and wanting to hear more.

Even if these questions are not asked by the investor, you might want to volunteer answers to likely questions in order to strengthen your discussion of this slide.

What's Next?

At the conclusion of this slide, you have used more than half your presentation time (about 12 to 15 minutes). You should have a much better idea whether the investor cares to hear more. As you move forward, try to adopt an even more casual and interactive style because the ice has now been broken (for better or worse). You should be working on improving your personal relationship and credibility with the investor.

If things are not going well, there is no shame in admitting defeat in this battle and calling a halt. The best way to terminate the presentation early is to understand why the investor is not biting and to seek an opportunity to re-engage after you do more homework. Always try to leave an open door no matter how poorly the presentation goes. Even if you are unsuccessful in gaining investor interest, you can still turn this meeting into a positive interaction by soliciting advice and seeking to learn insights that make your investment proposal more compelling to other investors.

But let's think positively—things are going well at this point and it's time to move on to the next slide.

Slide 7: Competitive Landscape

The Competitive Landscape slide (see Figure 14-1) summarizes how you are positioned against your current and potential competitors. It also provides an opportunity to demonstrate your knowledge of the overall marketplace and help convince investors that you have sufficient expertise in your area.

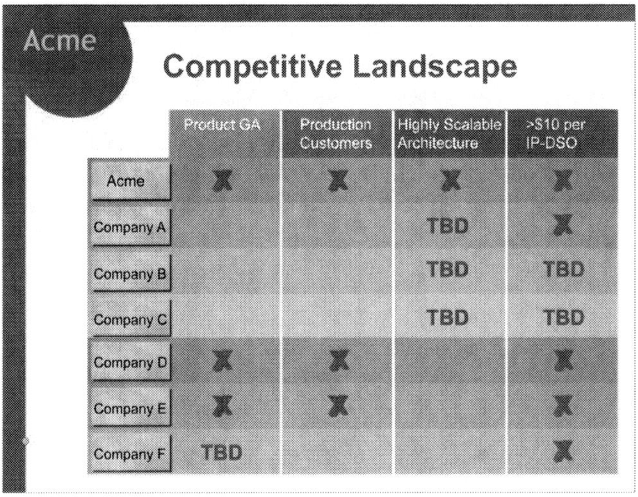

Acme — Competitive Landscape

	Product GA	Production Customers	Highly Scalable Architecture	>$10 per IP-DSO
Acme	X	X	X	X
Company A			TBD	X
Company B			TBD	TBD
Company C			TBD	TBD
Company D	X	X		X
Company E	X	X		X
Company F	TBD			X

Figure 14-1. A simple Competitive Landscape slide

An alternate title that works for this slide is "Market Landscape." With this title, you can include partners, potential acquirers, firms that you may want to be compared to, and, of course, competitors.

Focus on Why You Will Win

Start-up CEOs often say, "We have no competitors." This does not work in your favor and raises red flags. Investors believe that difficult problems in large, growing markets (i.e., where you need to be) attract competing solutions. They actually want to see some level of competition as a "space validator." Furthermore, investors expect their CEOs to maintain a healthy paranoia about possible alternatives and to be alert for changes in the market that could impact demand for their products.

Note   Stating that you have no competitors, even if true, is not a plus in the eyes of investors. They like to see some competition as a sign that there are, indeed, buyers in your market category. But they also like to see that you are keeping your eyes open for anyone with products that directly compete with yours, as well as peripheral products that might take care of market needs.

Even if you truly have no direct competition (for example, you have developed the first working time machine that allows travel back and forth in time), there are competing technologies and potential competitors that you could discuss to show your breadth of knowledge and to validate your space.

Pick your areas of comparison to provide a framework that highlight your major points of differentiation *the way that your key customers will see them*. In other words, make sure that you include buying-decision criteria that cause customers to buy your product over others. Avoid differentiators that are not highly correlated to the buying-decision process.

As an alternative, you may consider using the classic four-quadrant approach popularized by many large consulting companies, as shown in Figure 14-2. The five numbered circles represent five competitors and where they land on the cost/performance axis.

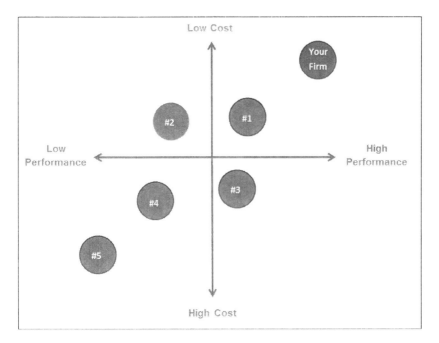

Figure 14-2. Classic four-quadrant competition slide

This approach can also be an effective format for your slide if customers have a limited number of key parameters that they evaluate when making purchase decisions. The four-quadrant approach has been (arguably) overdone, however, since its introduction back in the 1980s. Investors may be more receptive to seeing other, more comprehensive and creative graphics that are variations of Figure 14-2.

Tips on Developing an Effective Competitive Landscape Slide

Start the process by identifying your ideal target customers. This should primarily include larger, well-known, repeat buyers of your product if you sell to businesses, or well-defined groups of consumers if your products are sold to individuals. Recall from Chapter 9 that I presented a hierarchy of problems that customers seek to solve when they make purchase decisions. Business customers typically are attracted to solutions that help them increase revenues, lower costs, increase efficiencies, and entice more customers, among other things.

Consumers consider these criteria when making purchasing decisions, but they also consider products for reasons that are less financially oriented, such as items that provide enjoyment, create a sense of greater well-being, increase personal attractiveness, and so forth.

Once this data has been collected, construct a table that includes the most important buying criteria, along with the relative weighting of each feature *from the perspective of your target customer.* A simple form of such a table is found in Figure 14-3.

Features	myPhone 2	Rank	Competitor A	Rank	Competitor B	Rank	Competitor A	Rank
Cost	$399	8	$299	10	$425	6	$350	9
Screen Size	4.5 inches	10	4.0 inches	8	4.0 inches	8	4.0 inches	8
Battery Life	18 hrs	10	6.5 hrs	5	8 hrs	6	10 hrs	7
CPU	Atom X100	10	AMC 1.7 GHz	8	Zeta 4	9	Zeta 4	9
Weight	3.1 oz	10	3.5 oz	8	4.5 oz	6	4.5 oz	6
Memory	64 GB	8	64 GB	8	125 GB	10	64 GB	8

Figure 14-3. Competitor comparison matrix

The features in this chart, which relate to a new cell phone product and compared with competitors' products, are listed in order of importance to your customers' buying process. The ranking shown are based on a simple 1 to 10 scale. As with many other exercises in this book, you can overdo this analysis and get bogged down with unimportant details and features that may cause you and your team to lose sight of the forest for the trees and to waste precious time. Stick with the top four to six major differentiators, understand where you stack up, and how you compete—and then move on.

As you gather this data, it is also a good idea to set up a competitor database that is kept current by one of your employees. If your company is in a fast-moving space, you should have a formal competitor review meeting at least quarterly to review all the latest happenings and trends.

Be sure to use Google searches[1] to gather the latest information on all significant competitors, and then share noteworthy items with your staff. Some companies have a philosophy of discouraging frequent reviews of competitors in order to foster more creativity from their employees. With few exceptions (like maybe Apple), I have not seen this attitude produce successful teams. Andy Grove, the famous former CEO of Intel, encouraged his executives to maintain a healthy paranoia about their competitors[2] and to be fully aware of the market landscape of their products.

In any case, if you want to land external investment, expect to be grilled down to the minute details on how you will beat your competitors. CEOs who bury their heads in the sand, and who do not reflect a deep understanding of other solutions that customers may consider, rarely get to the finish line.

Tip   Appoint someone in your firm to keep tabs on new competitive products and new competitors. You always need to know where you fit in your category's "ecosystem." Investors will expect you to have this knowledge at your fingertips and will no doubt ask you questions about it to test you.

When this exercise is completed, it should be relatively easy to move the most critical and compelling elements of your analysis into a good Competitive Landscape slide. You will also be well prepared to answer questions that investors are likely to throw at you concerning how you stack up against competitive solutions. And remember, you are better off answering questions and concerns from customers' perspectives than offering your own opinions. Answers stated in terms that begin with, for example, "Our customers have given us the following feedback on the concerns that you raise," are much more powerful than first-person responses like, "I do not agree that [Product X] is much of a threat to us."

When all of your competitors have been rated, the results can be analyzed and ranked.

---

[1] Don't limit your research to Google searches. Ask customers what they think, attend industry trade shows, study web sites, interview current and former employees, and so forth.

[2] I highly recommend Grove's book, *Only the Paranoid Survive* (Doubleday, 1996). It presents many timeless insights on growing great companies and outfoxing competitors effectively.

How to Discuss Your Competition

In this section, I share some thoughts on how to talk about the Competitive Landscape slide, and what to emphasize and what to avoid.

It is common to hear pitches where the presenters take a "we're the greatest thing since sliced bread" approach, and largely brag about themselves while only giving lip service to competitors—and even then focusing exclusively on weaknesses. Again, this approach does not work well with investors.

As I have repeatedly emphasized, the fundraising pitch is more about the storyteller than the story. Your discussion of the competition and how you compare is very revealing about your nature, and contributes disproportionately to how investors size you up. Rather than boasting, you will be much better off making statements such as these:

- "While our customer feedback has been favorably consistent, we recognize that we have some holes to fill, and we are working hard to gain superiority in the following areas: ..."

- "Look, I will be frank with you. Our latest software release did not meet the expectations of several of our target customers. But, as a result, we have gained some important insights that will set us apart from our competitors. For example, ..."

Such "humble pie" approaches will help you build rapport with your investors and encourage more dialogue, which can prove to be critical in winning them over. Nobody expects you to have the perfect product with all the required bells and whistles when you are seeking an investment. However, they do expect you to be dead honest and to have a realistic assessment of what you have and what is still lacking.

Even if you have a full-feature set that already sets you ahead of most competitors, this slide provides an opportunity to discuss future product plans and to share unique customer insights that are leading you to develop novel differentiators—and not just copy and slightly enhance what others already have.

Tip Push yourself and your team to find a "10X differentiator"—something that is way beyond anything that your competitors have. Me-too products may be enough to land mom-and-pop investments, but investors looking for big returns will need to be convinced that you have something that is a game changer.

Guard against disclosing nonessential features just to show what your engineers have built. Investors know that many engineers are overly fixated on "polishing the apple" and tend to delay getting products out to customers for feedback. As famous business author Tom Peters' states, investors prefer to see a "ready, fire, aim" approach over one that overcooks products with excessive features. I think the pros of showing an investor that you understand how to be customer- and cost-focused far outweighs the "we're better at everything approach."

"We have no competitors."

Let's look more deeply into this since it's such a common sentiment among new entrepreneurs. Professional investors cringe when they hear fund seekers state that they have no competitors. An investor's first reaction is likely to be that…

- You have not done your homework.

- You are looking at your product far too narrowly and not considering other choices that customers might have (including not buying anything).

- Your target market is too small to attract other players.

- You are lazy and/or arrogant and breathing too much of your own air.

The overall experience that most investors have had reinforces the saying that "Pioneers are more likely to get arrows in their back than succeed." This really sunk in for those of us who invested too heavily during the dot-com area, when there were many start-up companies navigating the newly discovered Internet market for the first time. Claims of "no competition" were extremely common, and unfortunately, failure soon followed most of these firms—and investors sustained heavy and stinging losses. These days, few professional investors will invest in a company that professes to have no competitors.

Investors far prefer to see some level of competition because…

- The presence of competition helps validate that there is a large market.

- Competitors provide relevant benchmarks to allow more complete comparisons of industry business models.

- The presence of more players attracts more publicity and "buzz" that can elevate values.

- It is less expensive to launch a firm offering a concept that is already generally in demand. In other words, no expensive "missionary selling" is needed.

Let me go even further. If you are one of the rare companies that truly has no competition, you need to find some meaningful competition in order to provide comfort to your investor.

"Our competition is terrible."

Even if this is true, it is another comment that sends otherwise interested investors running for cover. So if you feel this way, you need to change your frame of mind; otherwise, astute investors will sense it by the way you come across—even if you do not use these exact words. You will be better received if you acknowledge at least some of the key strengths of your competitors, and then follow up by discussing how to effectively compete with them—and offer examples of customers who have selected your product over competitors.

Tip Avoid arrogance. There are many examples of brash and abrasive CEOs who delight in trashing their competition (especially when they were younger and less mellowed by harsh realities). Steve Jobs is a classic example. But he was a rare and very successful exception who does not make for a good role model. A humble-yet-confident approach is more much appealing to investors and better establishes your credibility. It also provides them comfort that they can work with you and that you will take and act upon their criticism, if needed. Arrogance is more a part of yesterday's style; it is less welcomed today.

Finally, as with other slides in this deck, save your backup slides (e.g., an analysis on each major competitor and competitive technology) for another meeting. However, you may want to mention that you and your team have significant backup materials available, which you look forward to sharing.

Lastly, watch your time. The discussion of competition sometimes takes on a life of its own. You need to carefully limit this initial discussion so that you can cover the remaining important points. Test out this slide with staff members and develop an approach to close the discussion. For example, you could say: "I'd be pleased to cover this area in more depth in a follow-up meeting," or, "Rather than diving into this more fully right now, can I send you our detailed competitive matrix and schedule a follow-up conversation?"

What to Expect

Experienced investors that are interested in a particular space will typically know quite a bit about competitive solutions, and they are generally more interactive during this slide than other slides. Definitely allow them to speak their mind, as the added interaction will help build your relationship with them—and you might even learn something! Their questions and insights will also allow you to size them up and determine where they might best fit. Let me elaborate.

Most of the investors that you are likely to interact with—especially in early investment rounds—will not be good candidates for board positions or provide significant added value outside the money that they invest. Nothing wrong with that—you are primarily looking for money, not advice. However, you will also encounter investors that potentially have much more to offer. These are true value-added types who can open doors, help you hire new employees, help make critical decisions, and so forth.

The interaction that you have with investors during this slide in particular can help you identify whether you have found an investor that can offer more than just money. The types of questions that they ask and the comments they make will help you determine (if you haven't already) whether or not they have relevant domain expertise. What's more, any enthusiasm they show in sharing insights on the competition, or challenging your perspectives, can help you decide if they may be potential board members, advisors, or fit in some other capacity.

While board members and advisors come in all flavors, those with strong domain expertise and a deep knowledge of competitors should be at the top of your list—and this slide can help you sort them out.

Slide 8: Go-to-Market Strategy

Slide 8, which describes your go-to-market strategy, tells investors how you plan to capture market share and grow your business. Even if you are not ready to launch your product, it is important to show your understanding of future sales and marketing strategies to establish that you, as CEO, have a comprehensive understanding of how to best generate future revenues.

If yours is a later-stage firm and already realizing revenues, this slide will be easier to develop and discuss. However, you still must convey to investors that you have a deep understanding of optimal revenue-generating strategies and can provide the leadership to achieve your sales projections.

As an investor, I am looking for CEOs who are totally in tune with growing sales—and who have excellent knowledge of how their marketing plans compare to similar strategies being employed by their competitors. If you lack deep comprehension of these areas, astute investors will quickly pick up on your shortcomings. Much like the Technology slide, which can be challenging for a marketing/sales-oriented CEO to deliver, Slide 8 can be tough for an engineering-oriented CEO to deliver. The good news is that if you carefully follow the steps in this chapter, you can successfully deliver this slide—even if sales and marketing are not your strongest suits.

Information to Include in This Slide

The Go-to-Market Strategy slide (see Figure 15-1a) typically includes the following information (listed by priority):

- The primary customers that you are targeting

- The channels that you plan to use (and their proportions) to access and support your target customers

- If you already have revenues, what you are doing today and how that will change

If you wish to show how your sales strategy will evolve from what currently exists, (pre-funding vs. post-funding), an overlay-type slide similar to the Technology slide example shown in Chapter 12 (Figure 12-1) can work well. This is the kind of slide where you show future changes by selecting components on the slide via a mouse-click.

Figure 15-1a is an example of a simple market strategy overview that allows you to verbally supplement the graphic elements with the names of customers and other information.

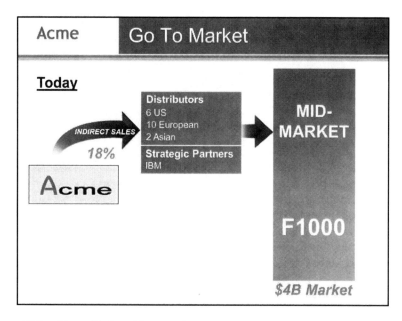

Figure 15-1a. Go-to-Market slide example

Anticipate this question: "In what ways is your marketing strategy different from your competitors?" Plan to provide an answer as part of a narrative on this slide. Figure 15-1b shows an example overlay slide presenting the changes planned for after the current funding round is completed.

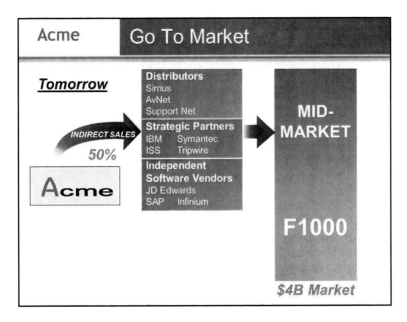

Figure 15-1b. Optional overlay slide showing future strategy post-funding

---

Note The use of overlay slides in your presentation can be very helpful. However, you need to be careful about the extra time that may be required to explain the added material. Technically, you are showing more than 12 slides, and you need to consider including some or all of the overlays in handouts if the file format that you share with your investors (e.g., a PDF file) does not allow them to mouse-click their way through the overlays.

Much like the Technology slide, this slide can invite a lot of questions and lead to a longer discussion. If such questions arise, first try to set a hook for a follow-up meeting. Second, be armed with a couple of backup slides that provide more details on likely follow-up questions. The most common follow-up questions typically include:

- Can you provide a detailed breakdown of products and services?
- Can you show me your pricing and margin assumptions?

- What are your promotional and marketing plans, and the related budget?

- What are your geographic expansion plans?

- How does your overall cost of sales compare to your competitors?

- Who are your top-five target customers?

- Can I see your latest sales forecast?

- What are your customer support strategies?

Prepare short, verbal responses to all of these questions and offer to provide more details during a subsequent meeting.

How to Develop This Slide

An effective slide is one whose simplicity reflects a lot of legwork and research. In this case, first go back to the data that you collected for the previous slide, the Competitive Landscape, and become thoroughly familiar with how your competitors distribute and support their products and services. If you have not done so, make sure your electronic competitor file folder contains information on each competitor's go-to-market strategy, including details on distribution partners.

Next, diagram the general distribution model used in your market segment, starting with your target customer and working backward to the competitors. Note the differences among competitors. Also note any new trends.

When it comes to marketing strategies, most firms tend to be followers. That is often the safest approach with investors, as changes to proven ways of attracting customers are viewed to be risky. If you are suggesting a new way of approaching customers, you might want to use the following example.

Let's suppose that you are selling online learning classes on technical topics (e.g., new programming languages, introduction to Windows 8, etc.) that provide continuing education to individuals. Your competitors market their products chiefly through e-mail campaigns using rented mailing lists. You are taking a different approach and plan to hire enterprise salespeople who will directly sell large annual contracts to companies to allow their employees to access your online courses. Using a variation of the overlay slide technique described earlier, your Go-to-Market slide first shows how your competitors go to market, and then, with a mouse click, it shows how you are different.

If you are innovating in an area, support your new approaches by verbally sharing feedback from actual or potential customers.

Tip   During our workshops, we often have our CEOs and their team members take an hour to map out the go-to-market strategies of their competitors on a white board or flip chart before starting on their own slide. Without fail, a significant number of firms told us that this exercise significantly changed their marketing approach. I highly recommend that you do this with your team.

Remember: Always Start with Your Customers

I have emphasized the importance of using a customer-centric approach in structuring your slides and related discussions. It is important that I expand on this topic relative to this slide since there are several "trapdoors" in how entrepreneurs handle this discussion, which can catch the unwary off guard and derail the pitch.

The biggest way to get off on the wrong track is to start Slide 8 without first discussing your target customers.

Many entrepreneurs start by emphasizing what their engineers are enthusiastic about and what they think would be cool and attractive to customers. Some groups also begin by sharing details of superficial customer surveys or anecdotal data from salespeople or other intermediaries. If this is or has been your approach, it will come out loud and clear on this slide—and you will be dead in the water from this point forward.

Caution   If you lead off any discussion with talking about what your engineers think are cool enhancements to your product, you are doomed. All that matters is whether customers think the product's features are useful and worth paying for.

You need to approach this slide after first having *significant* and *personal* quality interactions with your target customers regarding how they buy similar solutions. These interactions provide you with critical insights that savvy investors will recognize. Conversely, if you lack these experiences, you will raise red flags as you describe your strategy.

As a very important sidebar, a CEO needs to go out and rub elbows with key current and target customers every week. Do not leave these interactions to your sales or marketing people. Investors expect the CEO to be the top salesperson in a company—and the younger a company is, the more important this is. Remember, getting firsthand feedback from customers and potential customers will increase your credibility immensely when you stand before investors.

These days, most companies seeking funding are started by engineering geeks who naturally prefer to hang out with other engineers and technical types. There's nothing wrong with that. But if your business card reads "CEO," you are no longer just an engineer and you need to expand your skills, capabilities, and interests to include successful interfacing with customers. If you are too "geeky" when presenting this slide, and too limited in your ability to share personal customer interactions, you either will not get an investment, or as a condition of getting the investment, you will be quickly replaced with a more experienced CEO that has the skills.

Your research completed, you are now in a position to boil down your research and build an effective Go-to-Market Strategy slide. You will also have the market insights that will impress investors and further establish your credibility.

Let's now cover some best practices on how to deliver this slide.

Opening Remarks

Presuming that your plan is to generally mimic other successful marketing strategies used in your industry, the best opening for this slide is to start with something like: "Based on our[1] interactions with target customers, such as X, Y, and Z, and an analysis of our most successful competitors, we understand that customers prefer to purchase similar solutions through [describe the channel(s)]. Therefore, we have invested in developing our A, B, and C channels to map closely to the preferred buying behavior of our most desirable customers."

Then proceed to discuss the following:

- The mix of direct and indirect sales channels (more on this shortly)

- Critical sales/marketing partner arrangements now and in the future (with added emphasis if any of these partners may become future acquirers of the firm)

- Customer support strategies (with example cases)

- How much of your new investment dollars that you plan to invest in expanding sales channels

---

[1]Notice that this example opening starts in the second person plural ("our") and not in the first person ("my"). Minimize the use of first person references (I, my, mine, etc.). Investors view CEOs who are too self-centered as more difficult to work with. They far prefer team players who give credit to and share credit with others. The language you use in your presentation can reveal if you are in one category or another. Be careful and be sure to record yourself and seek critical comments from others (especially professional coaches) to tune the words and mannerisms that you use.

As mentioned, if you have developed a novel way to approach customers that may be a critical and an important differentiator, be sure you are prepared with strong validation and can cite specific customer feedback, and avoid a "build it and they will come" discussion.

The reality is that most successful companies do not start by making major innovations in go-to-market strategies. They focus their creativity on first developing superior products and services, and then utilize existing channel strategies to obtain their initial revenues. Your firm may be an exception, but investors will be skeptical. Just be careful and make sure you have validation if you are innovating in this area.

One certain thing about go-to-market strategies: they are always evolving as your firm matures. Investors understand this and will seek to understand 1) what you are doing today to reach and support customers, and 2) how that will change over the next three to five years. They want to see a credible vision of change based on your customer interactions.

■ **Tip** Plan on several iterations and avoid temptations to make this slide overly complex. As with the other slides, less is generally better. Don't let the slide content steal the center stage from you.

Channel Cost Considerations

Investors are often keenly interested in understanding the costs that are required to obtain and manage customers. They will also test your understanding by raising questions over your channel mix and want to get a sense that you have optimized costs. They know this is an area where excessively high costs can rapidly mount if not properly managed. While this subject matter is more detailed than what you will share on a first meeting, it is important that you understand several key concepts in the event that questions arise.

Let's start with basic concepts. Figure 15-2 shows a very simple sales distribution model showing common ways that firms connect with customers and vice versa. Due to the dramatic impact that Internet-based sales and marketing techniques have had on millions of businesses through lower costs and more efficient distribution models, investors are more sensitive than ever about the sales models used by the firms they invest in. If you are in a segment where the move to Internet-based sales and distribution is in process, expect to be asked some questions about its impact on your sales strategy.

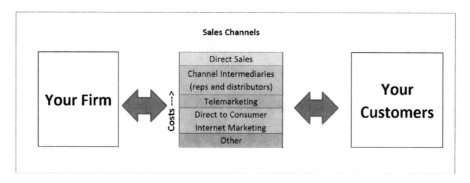

Figure 15-2. Basic sales channels model

As a CEO, you need to be conversant with your sales and marketing costs relative to that of your competitors, and to be able to position your firm as having at least a comparable sales channel model. It is not enough to simply know that your chief competitors are using, say, a mix of direct sales and Internet sales. You need to know the approximate ratio mix of sales channels and also the average costs of each channel that you and your closest competitors utilize (see Figure 15-3).

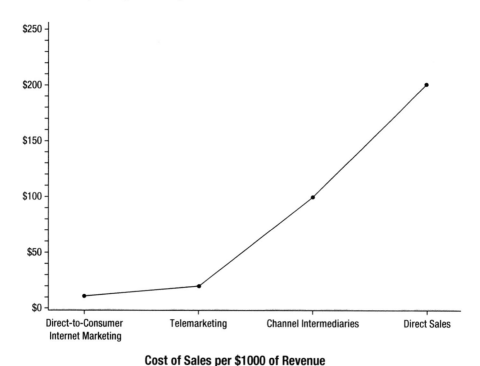

Figure 15-3. Typical sales costs for each $1,000 of revenue

Each channel has related costs/benefits that need to be balanced to provide an optimum distribution and support solution.

Due to extreme economies and the speed of performance provided by Internet-based strategies (e.g., you can buy a product on Amazon.com at a great price and have it delivered to your home the next day), this mode of accessing customers has become a game changer. As a result, investors will expect you to be at least on par with your chief competitors in using Internet distribution and support mechanisms for your products/services. Technology is rapidly changing in favor of even lower costs and new benefits, and this mode of marketing could develop into competitive advantages for your firm, which could be critical in attracting investor interest and funding.

Tip Make sure that you are competitive with other producers in using the Internet effectively to sell, distribute, and support your products. The Internet has revolutionized go-to-market strategies for nearly every kind of company, and investors will be looking to see that you are employing the newest Internet-based methods.

What to Expect

As the presentation moves forward, and provided that you ask questions to keep the investor engaged (e.g., "Do you have any issues with this slide?" or "Do you agree with our assumptions?"), you should be forming a better impression as to whether or not your investor is interested. It is rare that investors do not give you 20 to 30 minutes to make your pitch, even if they lose interest at some point before you are done. They did agree to meet with you, after all, and have already done some initial screening, so you can presume there was some general interest.

With each slide, you must either 1) build on that interest and work toward a next meeting, or 2) determine what you have said or shown them that cooled them. While the first objective is obviously desirable, the second objective is not a bad outcome provided you learn something valuable that makes your future fundraising more successful. The worst outcome is that you get through your presentation, think you have done a good job, and then fail to understand why you didn't get any follow-on interest.

You should now have a very good idea of how to develop and deliver an effective Go-to-Market Strategy slide. If you perform the recommended exercises with your team members, you will all also benefit from gaining a deeper understanding of the marketing and sales approaches used in your industry, which will be noticed and appreciated by potential investors. In short, you are now prepared to successfully cover this critical area and to move a step closer to a successful presentation.

I hope that I have also caused you to think more deeply about leveraging new technologies to better approach and service your customers. I did not even begin to touch on the use of social media, such as creating Facebook pages, using blogs, or setting up corporate Twitter accounts—but these are all things you should consider in order to improve your overall competitive advantages. As stated, investors are wary of investing in radical or unproven new ways to land and support customers, but including some cutting-edge approaches along with tried-and-true traditional techniques is positive and will be well-received.

Slide 9: Financial Road Map

An active professional investor receives hundreds of funding proposals a year, with many showing an average of more than $100 million in sales by Year 5. And most entrepreneurs state that their projections are conservative. As mentioned, if you are pitching a risky technology deal, $100 million is the amount that investors want to see.[1] As a result, that's the amount that they do see, including on your own Slide 9, the Financial Road Map.

So what do you do?

It's a tough nut to crack. If you show $20 million in sales by Year 5, they may believe it, but they won't write a check. If you show $100 million, they laugh to themselves—*unless* you have highly credible backup available, such as a track record of managing organizations of this size or some other advantage that lends your number some credibility.

---

[1] The ultimate objective with this slide is to strive match investor expectations/ requirements—and you need to do your homework in advance on what is needed to capture their interest. The figures in the examples in this chapter presume a high-risk, high-reward deal that might be attractive to a venture capitalist. If you pitching to an investor who has lower investment objectives, less aggressive projections may get the job done.

Creating Slide 9 is easy; proving that it is attainable is your challenge. The bottom line is this: if you want the money, you have to convey a big vision. Before I talk about that vision and challenge, let's focus on what goes onto this slide (see Figure 16-1).

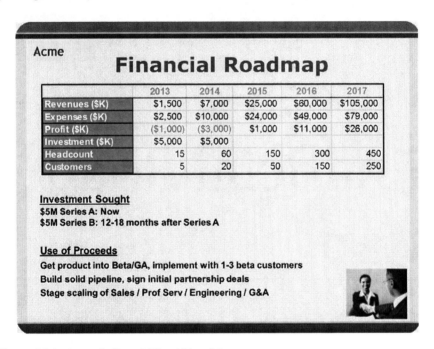

Figure 16-1. A sample Financial Road Map slide

As the slide demonstrates, you need to show five years of high-level projections for revenue, expenses, and profit. Depending on your situation, you may want to show employee headcount, number of customers, and so forth. Also show the capital required to reach your goals and what you'll do with the money. Highlight validation wherever you can (particularly from customers).

■ **Tip** Present your use of capital in terms of milestones. This ensures investors that you will put the money to good use. Examples might include: "Build customer base to 25,000 in three years" or "Establish sales pipeline into Canada in 12 months" or "Scale engineering to expand product line 50% within three years".

Investors tell us that they see far too many financial plans that aren't sound, consistent, substantiated, or comprehensive, creating an appearance of a lack of understanding of the dynamics of the business. Once you lose that credibility, you are toast. The rest of this chapter is about how to prepare sound plans that convince investors you know what you are doing.

What's Behind the Financial Slide

Should you drill down deeply into your operating plan in the first meeting? No. Plan for a simple overview but come prepared to address detailed questions—which you can expect—and show your understanding of the following topics:

- The business model and the economics of your business
- The company's revenue potential (from a market and a customer-centric perspective)
- The expenses required to run your business (validated with comparables)
- Your key assumptions regarding revenue potential and cost projections
- The path and timing to breakeven and to investor exit
- Cash flow—never forget that cash is king—and the timing and full magnitude of capital requirements (i.e., how much you really think you're going to need to achieve your goals and in what time frame)
- Your past financings and valuations
- A capitalization table showing both pre-money and post-money ownership positions

So make and record key assumptions related to all these items (and others, as appropriate), and build your income statement, balance sheet, and cash flow statement, making sure they all tie together. Make sure that you convey that you went through this process. You can and will get to the details during follow-up meetings.

You need to be able to discuss the implications of multiple scenarios and changing assumptions. That means you will need to develop an effective spreadsheet workbook that allows you to change high-level parameters and that provides accurate automatic updates of related details. It is an important tool[2] that you *must* have—and know inside and out (see Figure 16-2). If you can't build the detailed plan internally, seek outside help.

---

[2]There are various boilerplate versions of these types of workbooks available online. Local CFO groups are also a good source of templates. Invest time doing some Google searches before you attempt to create a workbook from scratch. Existing templates can save you time and are less likely to contain formula errors.

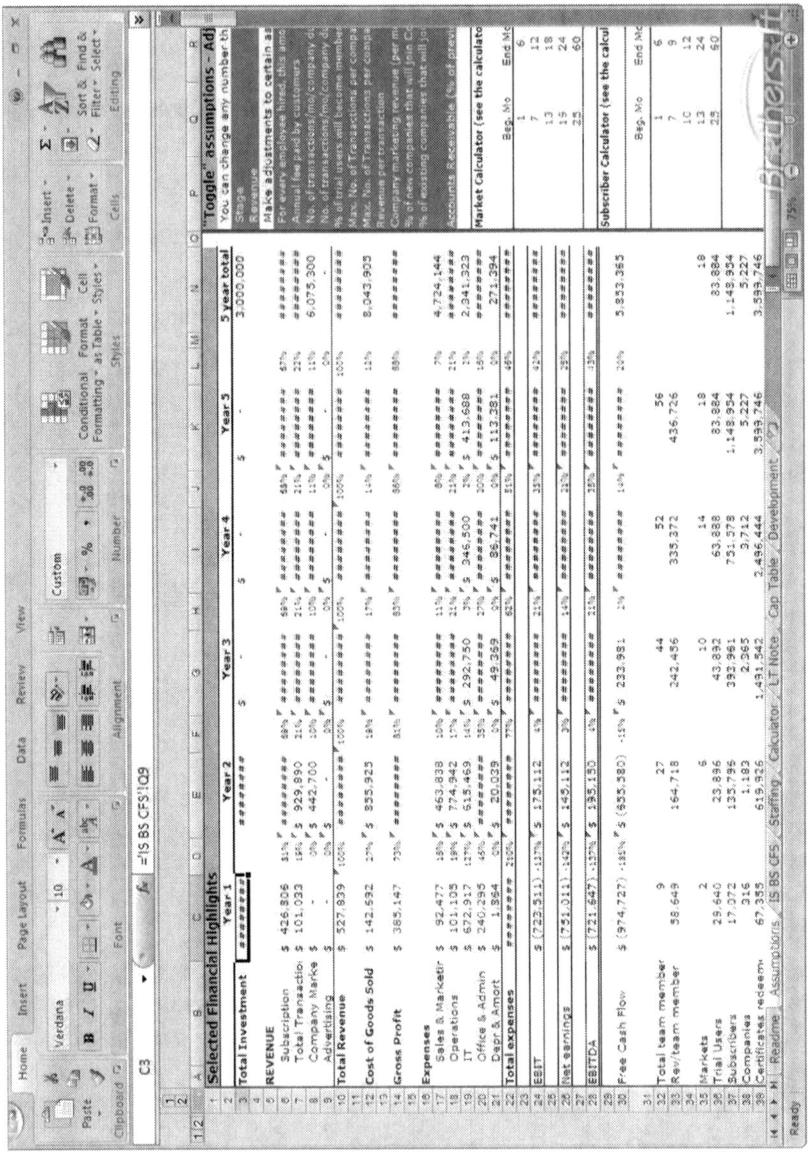

Figure 16-2. Sample financial model

The figures on the financial overview slide should be a roll-up of the detailed plan in your workbook. Be sure to mention that in your introductory remarks for this slide. In the unlikely event that the investors wish to go deeper and see something in your workbook, you should be prepared with a copy of this as background—but push to have a follow-up meeting where this can be discussed in more detail; otherwise, precious time will be lost on other important topics that need to be presented. (But take it as a good sign that they want more background here.)

TOP-DOWN AND BOTTOM-UP ANALYSES

A *top-down analysis* refers to the process of basing your projections largely on industry comparables. It is a useful first-order approximation that sets the stage for fine-tuning. A *bottom-up analysis* is derived from your internally generated data, including:

- Sales pipeline

- Revenue by customer

- Headcount

- Nonstandard cost ratios (e.g., your team decides to accept a larger proportion of non-cash compensation than other comparable firms)

- Nonstandard financings (e.g., use of grants, greater debt financing, etc.)

If you are an early-stage company and lack significant history, start with a top-down analysis and adjust it per your bottom-up analysis data. More mature companies can rely more heavily on bottom-up data, but make sure your assumptions are clear and valid.

Comparables

An often overlooked but very useful sheet in your workbook should contain cost ratios for your chief competitors, along with a comparative summary of how you stack up. Admittedly, this data may be difficult to obtain. Start with what you have and build on it over time as you learn more about your competitors. An easier place to get started is to look at public companies that are similar to your firm. Since these public companies may be larger than your firm, you can adjust their figures by making appropriate assumptions. Accounting firms that have experience with firms in your sector can also be an excellent source for obtaining this data. Investors want to see that your firm is paying attention to cost management, and the development of this worksheet as part of your model will be viewed very favorably.

Tip Having a spreadsheet that shows your financial projections compared with those of similar firms can be very persuasive. You'll need solid information, however—no guesswork or hopes and dreams.

Investment Sought

While your initial financial summary focuses on the current financing and funds sought, the current financing requirements need to be derived from your full future financing needs. Your detailed financial model should therefore project out to at least a breakeven point and show all past and future financings (equity and debt) that you anticipate needing to get there. Investors will also push you for detailed projections through a planned exit point for the firm (e.g., M&A or IPO). You might as well include this in your workbook. By developing a good sense of the "big picture," you will be much more confident in interacting with investors on this slide.

An important component to your projections is to understand the impact of planned financings on the ownership interests of the founder, investors, and other stakeholders. A detailed capitalization table, or "cap table," showing all investors and the value of their investments over time should be a part of the detailed workbook. It is unlikely, however, that you will get to this level of detail in an initial presentation. I stress the need to know this early because it will minimize surprises later, such as how you might be surprised by the level of ownership dilution that will occur when outside funds come into the company.

Due to many issues that investment funds had with investors during the financial meltdowns of the dot-com era and 2008 crash, fund managers are also wary of others that have invested. They want to avoid co-investing with relatively weak investors and/or people that may be antagonistic to their objectives. Prior to making an investment, fund managers thoroughly review your cap table and satisfy themselves that they can accept your prior investors—or they will pass on the deal. It is best to be prepared and present this information early, especially if you have any concerns that some of your current investors may not pass muster.

Use of Funds

How much you ask for and what you will do with the money are also derived right from your financial model. Discuss why you're seeking funds and list your top three uses for these funds, as well the approximate proportions to be allocated to each area. Be prepared to answer a common follow-on question: "How much cash will you need to get to breakeven?"

While we have seen many presentations where both too much and too little money is sought, most early-stage companies seek too little. There is a great tendency to be too optimistic about revenues and profits that will reduce the need for further funding rounds. It's best to be pessimistic, because things will likely take longer to develop than you expect and having more cash than you think you need will allow you to sleep better.

What to Expect

If the investor asks questions on this slide, consider that to be a good sign and a confirmation that you have maintained their interest to this point. A lack of interaction or questions is not good. You should initiate questions to uncover any issues (e.g., perhaps you lost everyone on an earlier slide). A couple of good questions to ask at this point: "Do these projections appear reasonable?" and "What other related information can we provide?" or "Would you be interested in reviewing our financial model and assumptions in more detail?"

To this point in your presentation, you should have planted the idea (and offered the validation) that yours can be a big play (big market, big need, differentiation, etc.). But, you will gain or lose credibility based on how sound your financial and business road map is. I would encourage you not to drill deeply into your operating plan details at the first meeting, unless you have to. Again, ask for a second meeting with finances as the main topic.

Don't forget: more important than what's on this slide is the process you go through to support it. It will be apparent if you have cut corners in doing research, talking to customers, and understanding the industry, or if you have failed to develop a financial workbook. And you will not get the money you seek until you have done the work that is required.

Go through the process outlined earlier and make sure that it all ties together, and convey that you went through such a process in preparing this slide. Plus, be sure to mention that you can and will go into deeper details at later meetings.

Slide 10: The Team

The process of presenting the team often begins well before a first meeting. Prior to a first meeting, professional investors may visit your web site and look at the general backgrounds of your team members. They may also check with their colleagues or other investors to learn more about the backgrounds of your key executive staff members. The pre-screening process is made even easier these days through the use of social networking sites such as LinkedIn and Facebook.

MAKE A GOOD FIRST IMPRESSION

When it comes to making good first impressions, do not overlook the significant impact that social media can play. Take the time to look at the web profiles of your key executives, and then have them make adjustments to optimize the impression that they convey to investors. You need to encourage them to shift from "friend-making" mode to portraying a professional image that will impress investors. Be forewarned that this process may create some friction—not unlike telling someone that their choice of dress or hairstyle is not appropriate.

Also, expect that some may feel that you are overreaching into their personal lives when you ask them to remove photos of themselves drinking margaritas in Cabo with a bunch of fellow partygoers.

Start with LinkedIn profiles because this site is more oriented to professional profiles. But look at other sites, such as Facebook, and make sure that there is nothing that would trigger investor concerns.

As has always been the case, first impressions are still extremely important. The founding team is one of the most important aspects in the investor's mind. An investor will size you up during the pitch by judging how you present and how you answer questions and provide information that is not on a slide. Your personality, natural intelligence, and ability to charm them with your vision will be on center stage.

The team, particularly the CEO, is evaluated from the second you walk in the door. Most investors say they like to "bet on the jockey, not the horse." They want you to demonstrate that you can pull off whatever big idea you have and that your team in itself is a competitive advantage.

First and foremost in Slide 10, The Team (see Figure 17-1), you want to emphasize relevant track records in the target domain, as well as the skills that you and your team bring to the table. Ideally, investors will also want to see recognizable names—people or companies—in the listing of the board of directors.

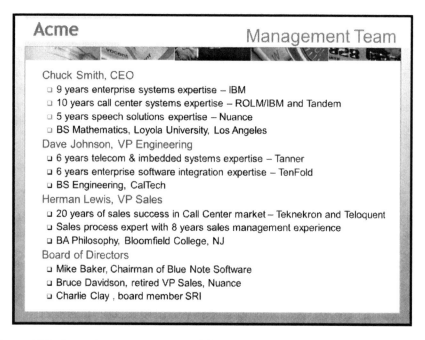

Figure 17-1. A sample management team slide

Ideally, most investors want to hear some of the following six comments from CEOs in regard to their team:

- *"We have many of years of experience, and we have spent many years in this space."* Investors want to invest in industry experts who have a strong personal network of market segment–related contacts. Be sure to emphasize each key team member's relevant history, including your own.

- *"We have worked well together multiple times in our careers."* Investors love to hear that you and at least some key staff members have worked closely before. They know that growing companies can create friction in the ranks, and prior history of working together is viewed as very favorable.

- *"We have worked for big-name companies and have also been successful as entrepreneurs."* Investors want to see that key team members have prior experience working in larger firms. Such experiences reinforce that you have been exposed to best practices, well-developed systems, and infrastructure, which will minimize learning curve risks as you grow your company.

- *"We have appropriate, well-respected credentials."* Think degrees from respected schools. Investors associate academic credentials with a greater likelihood of success. A big mistake that is a silent deal-killer is when a CEO who lacks a degree intentionally omits the degrees of team members, thinking that this will not call attention to his personal lack of credentials. Any listing of team members without degrees is a sign to many investors that the CEO is a nonstarter who lacks appropriate credentials.

- *"We have already attracted high-quality seed investors and board members."* As a sign that some prior validation has occurred, professional investors want to be sure that you have attracted other quality investors and advisors. There are rare exceptions in which a highly compelling story can overcome this; but don't count on it. Before you go hunting for larger investments, get well-recognized people connected to your company as early investors or advisors.

- *"And, most importantly, we have made money for investors previously."* Although this is the toughest claim of all, it is a huge plus if you can make it. Even if you as the CEO cannot say it, work extra hard to attract team members who can—and help develop the perception that you have a winning team. This is even more critical if your last deal lost money. Losing money is not the end of the road, since investors understand there are more losers than winners, but they want to feel comfortable that you have a team that has at least some solid experience in winning deals.

Investors are also expecting you to be frank and honest about any key executive "holes" that you have and how you plan to fill them. Good investors have extensive networks of qualified entrepreneurs. Sometimes they can help you fill a hole on your team—and become more committed to your investment opportunity.

GET THE BEST

A recent deal that we looked at originated from ideas that a brilliant young engineer from the University of California, Berkeley developed while still in graduate school. He was smart enough to follow the wise advice of his mentors to seek more mature and experienced team members to join him in building a new company—even people who were significantly older than he was. I was all the more impressed when I met with the full team and saw what a terrific job the young engineer had done in picking highly experienced and compatible team members to help him realize his vision. His team members' credibility, track record, and prior investor contacts ensured the success of the firm in raising needed capital. Today they are well on their way to achieving a very profitable outcome for their firm.

Unfortunately, this story is more of an exception. It is much more common to see an inexperienced CEO surround himself with similar inexperienced people—and then hope that investors will get excited because their idea is so cool. If you are in your 20s or early 30s, be sure to be very objective about the team that you assemble and present to investors. Some gray hair on the team can be a big plus.

As I mentioned several times, part of your homework before the presentation is to find connections between you and your key executives and the investor group that you are meeting with. Any important connection points that will help the investor validate you and your team are worth mentioning. However, beware of excessive name-dropping. Making too much of an effort to mention people you know for the sake of showing how connected you are can backfire and make you look shallow or lacking in self-confidence. So pick those names carefully and use them sparingly in your presentation.

The Slide Format

The curriculum vitae (CV) format works well for this slide, as shown in Figure 17-1. Simply list jobs, companies worked for, and relevant schools attended. There is a trend to show energetic and friendly group photos of the team, and using only minimal text on the slide, while the CEO goes over the CV details ("That's Dave Johnson on the far left. After graduating from Caltech, he…") This approach works best when you expect that the investor has already done preliminary research on you and your team (which happens most of the time these days). Figure 17-2 provides an example.

Figure 17-2. An alternate, and increasingly common, team slide format (slide courtesy Gauss Surgical)

Most presentations work best when this team slide is presented toward the end of the deck, as it is here. However, if you feel you have an "A" team—for example, well-known executives, board members, and investors from previous rounds—move it near the front. The strength of the team often trumps the concept, especially if you are an early-stage firm without much history. Remember, investors prize prior start-up success above most anything else. So if you are that good, emphasize it early.

 Tip   If your team is truly stellar—brilliant people, successful entrepreneurs, top-grade angel funding, or what have you, move up this slide in the presentation to the second or third position. It will set a positive tone for the rest of the meeting.

Lastly, be prepared to emphasize what *you* bring to the table. The CEO is the most critical team member, and you must summarize your value and show that your unique mix of skills and abilities can make money for investors in a convincing manner. It's OK to brag about your past successes—just keep it relevant, factual, and low-key.

There is a fine line between boasting and recapping prior successes, and this is difficult for many entrepreneurs to realize. In many coaching sessions, we find ourselves toning down the presentation style of our CEOs—especially on this slide. As important as it is to emphasize prior successes, err on the side of underplaying this area. Realize that most professional investors have done their homework and already know something about you and your team members. An understated humble approach works best. Let your accomplishments speak for themselves.

What to Expect

If you have assembled a good team with prior experience and appropriate credentials, this slide can be one of the easiest ones to present. On the other hand, this slide will be the end of the road if it causes investors to believe that...

- Neither you nor your team has been around the block yet.

- Your ability to attract stars is lacking.

- You will be outgunned by more experienced competitors.

To ensure a favorable reaction to this slide, review and internalize those six comments that investors want to hear, as summarized earlier in the chapter. You do not need to make all of these points to keep investors interested, but try to develop at least three areas that fit your team.

Also, be sure to mention any "holes" in your team. No investor expects you to have the perfect dream team in place—especially at earlier funding stages. If you mention an executive hole that you plan to fill with funds from the next financing round, and the investor can help you fill it, it may create more interest in funding your deal and give you another hook for getting follow-on meetings and interactions.

I have stressed that investors often consider the people in your deal more important than just about anything else. If your presentation has only gotten "so-so" interest up to the prior slide, who and what you present on The Team slide can get you back on track.

Slide 11: Current Status

Like the other the slides, Slide 11, Current Status (see Figure 18-1), is important. There are three important objectives to accomplish with this slide:

1. Provide a report card to investors indicating what you have accomplished with prior funding.

2. Reinforce your accountability for setting goals and achieving objectives.

3. Provide a preview of the high-level summary reporting that investors can expect to see from you to show the progress made in your plan from using their invested funds.

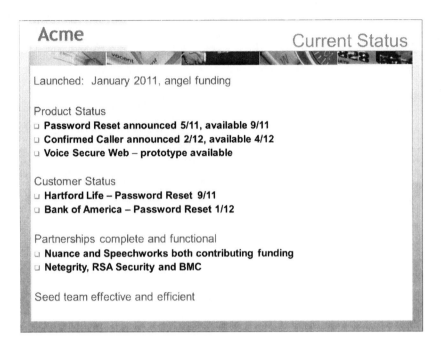

Figure 18-1. A simple summary of Current Status

A common problem that investors encounter is a lack of follow-up after they have written a check. Indeed, this is probably the biggest complaint that I hear from fellow investors—and something they are all extremely sensitive to when it comes time to evaluate new investments. You need to be aware that when investors are checking references, one of the first questions they ask is: "Were you pleased with the frequency and thoroughness of the reporting that you received after investing with this entrepreneur?" And then they'll ask a follow-up question: "Does this entrepreneur have a good track record with meeting committed objectives?"

Rightly or wrongly, investors perceive that many (most?) entrepreneurs are sloppy about managing and monitoring progress against objectives. They also believe that it is very difficult for individuals who have previously demonstrated a lack of attention in this area to change their behaviors just because a check has been received. While rarely voiced as an explicit question during an initial presentation, I assure you that investors will be sizing you up and determining if you are an exception. By emphasizing diligent reporting and a relentless drive to deliver on expectations, you will build their trust in you.

When you present this slide, you must convey that you relish being held accountable and that you maintain high personal standards in managing your team to meet expectations. The best way to accomplish this is to once again provide storytelling that expands on what you have listed on your slide.

Note Surprisingly, many investors feel shut out after they have written a check. Therefore, you must provide regular reports to your investors on progress made, milestones hit, customers gained, revenues increased, and so forth. Also, don't forget investors are smart people. In most cases, they will be happy to provide advice when you need it.

What to Report on This Slide

Let's first discuss the general areas that investors want to see covered, and then drill down with some examples on how you can deliver a winning performance. The top areas that investors wish to receive status reports on include:

- Products
- Customers
- Partnerships
- Team updates
- Progress against previously committed financial objectives, including discussions of any significant variances, use of capital, and so forth

Once you have received funding, the top priority—and typically the first topic that is reported and commented on, is your financial performance. It often focuses on the use of funds, burn rate,[1] and related variances. However, in this first presentation with a new investor, comments on the other areas that I listed should be the primary focus (see Figure 18-1).

Products

While it is important to summarize the status of your products and services at the time of the presentation, in order to highlight your accountability and ability to drive results, you should include brief comments on how your team

---

[1] A burn rate is the amount of cash that you are consuming per reporting period, which is usually monthly. It is often the first and most important aspect of the financial parameters that investors want you to present. They want to see that your spending is in line with expectations and that you are doing an effective job squeezing the most out of your available funds.

performed on previous objectives. Using the slide shown in Figure 18-1, your product status narrative might include the following:

> *We have succeeded in meeting our committed objectives on key milestones this past year, including delivering the Password Reset and Confirmed Caller features. We also completed a web-based Voice Secure prototype two months ahead of schedule, even though we experienced delays from our third-party manufacturing firm. This has allowed us to accelerate beta tests at key accounts.*

Notice how this discussion relates more to the process than the result, which confirms to the investor that you are delivering against objectives and taking pride in achieving/beating estimates. This is much more effective than providing your current product status by merely stating the following:

> *Our product currently includes Password Rest and Confirmed Caller features and we have completed a Voice Secure web-based prototype.*

Customers

Regardless of what round you are raising, you should include two to three customer status–related bullets. Even if you have not interfaced with customers, your bullets should state your plans to gain needed input. Here is an example of a good short narrative related to customer status:

> *Earlier this year, we targeted both [Fortune 500 insurer] and [Fortune 50 bank] as highly desirable targets for beta-testing our new features. This quarter, we have succeeded in receiving beta-test agreements from both firms, which will move us closer to generating our first revenues early next year.*

Contrast this summary with a weaker snapshot-type summary:

> *[Fortune 500 insurer] and [Fortune 50 bank] have agreed to beta test our new Password reset feature.*

Partnerships

While new partnerships are generally further down the totem pole in terms of what investors deem important, progress in this area with well-known partners who have a direct impact on revenues and costs can be effective to highlight—especially if the status came about as a result of a planned effort with set objectives.

An effective narrative on the status of partnerships might include the following:

> We are ahead of schedule in obtaining commitments from [two Fortune 1000 tech companies] to participate in the current funding round, subject to terms received from a lead investor. This year's business plan included landing at least one of these firms as a strategic investor, and I am pleased to report that we got both of them to step up. We also achieved our objectives for securing marketing agreements with [Fortune 1000 tech companies] after beating out our chief competitors in a bake-off by all three firms.

Team Status

Since you already presented an overview of your team, use this slide to cover team items related to achieving hiring objectives and dealing with any personnel issues. The following is an example of a good narrative for this area:

> We have completed all hiring objectives for our seed team, and judging by our effectiveness in hitting milestones, we are well on our way to establishing a very results-oriented company culture, which is one of my top personal objectives. We are continuing to have challenges, however, in locating a suitable candidate for a quality control position, which we plan to add next quarter. We would appreciate your suggestions.

The topics that we just covered are by no means the only areas that you should cover. Feel free to substitute other topics that may be more relevant to your industry, including:

- Patent filings
- Government approvals (e.g., FDA approval of a medical product)
- Technology milestones

However, make sure that the topics closely relate to either revenue generation or customer validation, as these topics interest investors the most. Also, select achievements that came about as a previously planned activity—not something that occurred just by happenstance. You want to hammer home how you have repeatedly set and met—and/or exceeded—past objectives.

I hope that you now understand and can replicate the style of narrative that will deliver a good performance of this slide!

▧ **Tip** In your presentation, always look for reasons to tell a story. They not only convey important points, but they hold the investor's interest more than a simple recitation of facts.

What to Avoid

The Current Status slide is one that establishes your ability to deliver meaningful results in a timely manner and to indicate that you have a disciplined and predictable reporting style that can be relied on. However, you can compromise these objectives by overly discussing future plans, or by avoiding a discussion of solid accomplishments in past plans.

Stick with describing what you have now. Emphasize the role of the planning process and the team's ultimate performance in prior plans.

A Question that Might Come Up

A good question to anticipate and be prepared to answer during the presentation of this slide is: "What do you plan to accomplish in the future?"

Should this question come up (and assume it will), try to use this as another hook for a second meeting by providing the following answer: "I would be pleased to share our future plans in detail with you, but would prefer to do this in a follow-on meeting where I can share our assumptions and get your input and suggestions. Would that be OK?"

We have found that a discussion of future objectives is best accomplished after an investor has heard and absorbed the other, more fundamental information that you have presented—and agreed to have a follow-on meeting with you.

Here is what can go wrong if too much discussion of future objectives takes place in the first meeting:

- Information overload and loss of interest in a follow-up meeting because the investor believes there is nothing more to be gained.

- Your future plans will be a function of how much you raise in current and future rounds. If you are still raising money, there will be greater uncertainty about what you can realistically achieve—and you may set unrealistic objectives that can impact your credibility.

- Many professional investors want to be able to provide input to help shape your future direction and they may react negatively to a firm road map that appears to be cast in concrete.

- Finally, things change. While you need to convey that you have a solid vision of where you want to lead the firm, presenting too much detail on specifics—especially those that are beyond what can be accomplished during the current funding round—can reflect indifference to future input that you might receive from customers, investors, and advisors.

If you are pressed for a slide on future plans, make it as general as you can and still set a hook for a follow-on meeting. Figure 20-1 in Chapter 20 shows a slide that you might adapt.

What to Expect

You are now nearing the end of this important initial investor meeting, and provided that you have maintained interaction with the investor, you should now have a very good idea of their interest in taking next steps. If the investor remains interested at this point, they will agree to a follow-on meeting to discuss your plans and other items that hooked them in earlier slides.

Now let's move on to a strong finish!

Slide 12: Summary

Remember, the primary objective of the first meeting with investors is to get a second meeting. Your goal in the Summary slide is to continue the positive momentum that you have established, while providing added due diligence and developing rapport with the investor. In this last part of the presentation, you want to do the following:

- Summarize your strongest points
- Reiterate synergies and common objectives that you have with your investor
- Obtain investor feedback
- Deliver a call to action

Slide 12, the Summary (see Figure 19-1), is your opportunity to end on a memorable note. On this slide, summarize your three or four strongest points—distilled down to memorable sound bites. The top areas that grab investor attention include:

- A strong team with proven ability to deliver results (Team)
- A big and growing market opportunity (Market)
- Customer validation that you have a solution they prefer (Product)
- Credible business projections that will deliver required returns (ROI)

Figure 19-1. A sample Summary slide

If you delivered your previous slides based on my suggestions, you should have adequately covered these key areas, so you need only to lightly summarize them here. Then shift the discussion into a recap of potential synergies with prospective investors. For example, you can discuss how you'd fit into their portfolio, how their background relates to your business sector (such as their applicable domain expertise), why you think they would make a great addition to your team, and so forth.

At this stage, solicit feedback and ask the investor to honestly summarize any areas of potential concern. Even if concerns were brought up during your earlier slides, ask that they be summarized once again. This will give you a better idea of the priorities of their concerns. It's best to get a candid summary—including all problem areas—while your pitch is still fresh in front of them; otherwise, you may waste needless energy speculating on why they did not call you back. If there are multiple people in your audience, also try to draw out the opinions of other key investors. Some good questions to ask include:

- Can you summarize any of your concerns or issues with what I have presented?

- Where do you think I need to do more homework?

- Do you have any suggestions to make my presentation more effective?

- Is there anything that I missed that you have not shared with me?

Call to Action

You will know that you had a successful first meeting with the investor if you cement interest in specific follow-up steps that you commit to take together. Summarize all the hooks (i.e., areas where the investor raised concerns or wanted to see more data) developed from interacting with the investor during the previous slides; for example, you could say: "You indicated that you were interested in obtaining more information about our technology road map, as well as seeing our sales pipeline."

Push to get a commitment to allow you and your team members to present more information and to determine potential times for a follow-up meeting: "Are you available for a follow-up meeting within the next ten days so that we can present this data and obtain your feedback?"

If you cannot get a firm commitment for a next meeting, at least determine what it will take to get that meeting. More face time is best, but even if you leave with their commitment to review additional items that you will provide via e-mail, that is also a good outcome.

Take the lead in providing a tight summary of next steps. Emphasize what you are committing to do and when you will get it done. Don't be overly aggressive in setting a deadline for yourself. Saying that you will deliver requested items "in the next couple of days" is better than saying, "I will have these items to you by noon tomorrow," which will put added, unnecessary stress on you/your team to deliver. It's best to "under commit and over deliver."

HOW PUSHY SHOULD YOU BE?

Investors know that you are trying to raise money and that you do not want to waste time on dead ends. They expect you to close with them by requesting next steps. It is far better to "cut to the chase" and close the meeting by asking for another meeting than to not. You are the chief sales guy for raising your round, and if you leave on a meek note, you will weaken your first impression.

Caution Professional investors are not likely to commit to an investment in the first meeting, so one question to avoid asking is, "Can I count on you to provide an investment?" While this type of closing may work with angel investors or friends and family, professional investors typically make investments only after performing deep due diligence over multiple meetings. And then they make a final decision based on feedback from their internal investment committee. You can, however, ask the following: "From what you have heard so far, does our company generally fit your investment criteria?" Although if you ask for and get confirmation of interest in a follow-up meeting, this question is redundant.

What to Expect

Close by thanking investors for their time and interest. Offer a solid handshake and good eye contact. Leave the room with a confident demeanor. Don't forget to say good-bye to the office manager and other support staff; they may become important in helping you set up meetings to follow.

You can gauge the success of your meeting by the level of commitment from the investor to take next steps. The best outcome is having a firm date and time for the next appointment. Even if you are unable to secure a next meeting, you will have gained significant new information that can either allow you to rekindle interest with this investor or further tune your pitch to new investors.

Backup Slides

Since you can never be sure how an initial presentation may go, it is important to prepare backup slides that support the 12 Magic Slides. Before we discuss typical backup slides, let me offer a few words of caution:

- Don't forget that the primary goal of a first meeting is to get a second meeting. Before offering backup slides to answer questions, try to leverage investor interest in obtaining more data by first asking if they would be interested in a follow-up meeting.

- If you do need to offer backup data, try to provide this information verbally without the use of additional slides. If you absolutely need to show other slides, keep them limited because you may compromise the time needed to cover your primary slides.

- Having too many backup slides in your initial presentation deck can weaken your presentation and get you off track. Having fewer slides allows you to spend more time talking and sharpens your focus in making each of the basic 12 slides as effective as possible.

With these caveats in mind, let's discuss the typical backup slides that you should prepare.

Future Timeline Slide

The Future Timeline slide (see Figure 20-1) is a must-have backup slide. It might even make it into your initial presentation, time permitting. This slide can be a very powerful way to show how you envision...

- Utilizing investment funds from this round.

- Solving any critical product gaps.

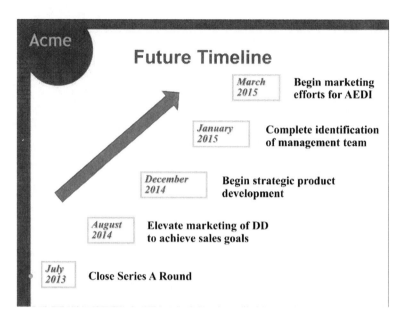

Figure 20-1. Perhaps the most useful backup slide—the Future Timeline

Also, it is a good place to underscore that you have future offerings planned—and that you are not just a "one-trick pony."

If you present some form of this slide, be sure to set a hook for a follow-up. So resist any temptation to spill all of your future plans in a first meeting. Do not dwell on details and try to return to your core slides as quickly as possible. A good way to close on this slide and get back on track might be to say something like: "Here is a very high-level future timeline of our current plans. Over the next 24 months, our primary objectives are to [state up to three]. I would be pleased to go over our assumptions and would also appreciate receiving your input and feedback during a follow-up meeting. Would that be of interest to you?"

Disclosure Slide(s)

I strongly encourage you to include a disclosure slide to follow the opening title page. In practice, CEOs often click through these slides and do not say much more than: "This presentation is subject to standard disclosures that all investors should review before making any investment." (That's why I'm not counting it as one of the Magic 12.)

The language in the slide shown in Figure 20-2 is quite common. Be sure to have your attorney review and/or suggest language that may be appropriate for you.

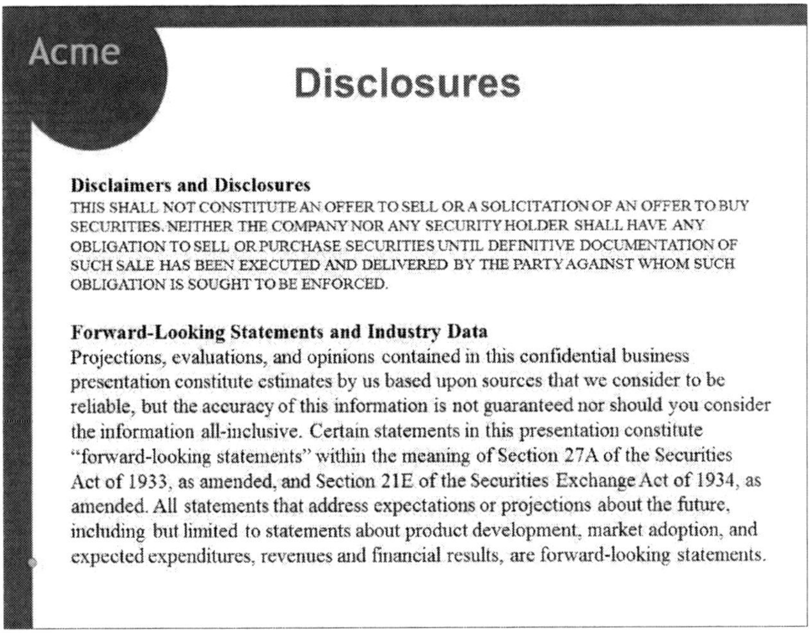

Figure 20-2. A standard Disclosure slide

When should you use disclosure slides? I recommend using them whenever you are making a presentation whose purpose is to obtain funding for your company. If you are simply presenting an overview of your company to interested individuals (e.g., customers, prospective employees, advisors, etc.) for information purposes (and not seeking their investment), a disclosure slide is not necessary.

While many presentations do not contain a disclosure slide, and some advisors would even suggest that it is not needed for an initial presentation, why take a chance? The addition of a disclosure slide does not materially impact the time to cover your other slides and signals to investors that you are taking a more conservative approach in sharing initial information with them.

Other Backup Slides

I also recommend having a limited number of additional slides prepared to provide additional information for the following:

- **Solution slide:** Prepare alternate views that more fully show your solution. A short video (1 to 2 minutes) of a customer using your solution can be very effective.

- **Technology slide:** If your slide deck includes a simple technology overview, have a more detailed version available to cover major areas. Use overlays that you can click through. Another good backup slide is a summary list of completed and pending patents.

- **Financial Roadmap slide:** While I do recommend completing a full financial workbook (as discussed in Chapter 16), I suggest that you do no more than show the first sheet along with labeled tabs of the other worksheets. The discussion of your financial assumptions and your various worksheets is definitely outside the scope of a first meeting—and you will get seriously bogged down if you get into your workbook during this time. Backup slides could include a high-level sales projection, a headcount plan, sources and uses of funds over the near term (12 months), and possibly profit margin projections if you plan significant cost reductions.

With the caveats that I outlined, you may or may not show these slides in your initial presentation. Anything beyond what is outlined here needs to be saved for a follow-on meeting.

After the Meeting

The meeting has now ended. You have a good feeling about investor reaction to your presentation. They expressed interest in following up and have asked for additional items, which you believe is an indication that they wish to continue their discussions with you.

What happens next?

Your high-level objectives are to accomplish the following:

- Take steps to continue and further increase interactions with the investor.

- Build interest through periodic sharing of positive information about your company (e.g., new customers, product enhancements, new hires, important customer feedback, etc.).

- Work toward setting up follow-on face-to-face calls to allow deeper analysis of your business opportunity.

- Maintain your cool and don't oversell or get too pushy— be steady, but patient.

In Your Car After the Meeting

Immediately after the meeting—even in your car in the parking lot, before details begin to slip away—take the time to write down all of the action items that came out of the meeting. If the meeting went well, with good investor interaction, and you volunteered follow-up materials, list all of your commitments as well as any other items that may be helpful in answering questions and providing more interest in your firm.

When you get back to your office, write an immediate follow-up e-mail to thank prospective investors for the meeting (copy the investor's administrative assistant—she or he can be very helpful going forward). In the e-mail, address any unresolved issues, and stress points that resonated. Also, recap actions items and provide a timeline for when you can deliver them (save the actual delivery of specific items for separate follow-on e-mails or meetings).

Next, reconnect with your referral sources and brief them on how the meeting went. If appropriate, have them contact your investor(s) for their feedback as well. If you have been asked to provide references, be sure to contact them in advance and coach them on what you would like them to say.

Finally, begin to create opportunities for follow-up: offer to provide references if you haven't, ask to meet other partners, interact with other companies in the investors' portfolio companies, or provide a technology, financial, or sales pipeline review.

Within the Week

Within a week, begin efforts to firm up the next face-to-face meeting. Investors are busy, and if they don't hear from you, well, "out of sight, out of mind." Be persistent in a friendly way until you get another meeting or a no.

Here are some realities that you need to keep in mind in order to set realistic expectations on how next steps may evolve:

- Investors will typically not follow up unless you or your ideas are very hot and there is urgency in making an investment decision.

- Regardless of what the investor committed to do, presume that the ball is in your court and that you are solely responsible for driving next steps.

- Fundraising and related due diligence gathering is a slow process. Often, 90 days or more may elapse between a first meeting and having fresh money in the bank.

Professional investors are often inundated with deals and also have other responsibilities—such as sitting on multiple boards, raising money for new funds, and so forth—that consume a lot of time. Once your meeting ends, in spite of everyone's best intentions, the details about your presentation will fade as other work encroaches.

So don't expect an unprompted e-mail or phone call in the week after the presentation. Just as importantly, don't assume that a lack of follow-up means a lack of interest.

▓ **Note** Just because you don't hear from the investor in the days or weeks after the presentation doesn't mean they are not interested. Most likely, they simply have a lot on their plates that demand their attention before contemplating your deal further.

Next Steps

After you have completed all initial follow-up actions, including requests for follow-up meetings, and presuming that you have not received a hard "We're not interested," it is important that you stay in at least weekly contact. Too often, entrepreneurs abandon interactions with investors if they do not receive responses to follow-up communication. Don't allow yourself to succumb to that behavior. Instead, do each of the following items discussed…

Update Your Investor List

Scrupulously maintain your investor status spreadsheet (see Figure 3-2) and review it each day to determine what other steps can be taken to continue at least weekly communication with investors who have not given you a firm "not interested." It is a good practice to put a date next to each note, which summarizes the interaction (e-mail, phone call, etc.), so that you can quickly identify any lapses in communication that extend beyond one week. In the spreadsheet, be sure to include any junior people that attended your presentation, because they may be easier to contact.

Press for Follow-up Meetings

Always press for follow-up meetings. Additional face-to-face meetings are the best means of obtaining an investment—or in learning why there is no interest to invest. One of our objectives in only presenting 12 slides, you may recall, was to "leave them wanting more." Now is the time to deliver your more comprehensive technology, finance, or sales story.

By now, if you're in a normal VC or angel process, three to six weeks might have passed. If you know that the best VC processes can take three to six *months*, you won't feel the time pressure. If you left funding to the last minute, you'll need to be more aggressive, which is a shame. But, either way, your next step is to find a reason for the investor to see you again. This could be due to a major new release of the product and "I'd love to show you because I think you'll find it interesting." And you promise to stay only 20 to 30 minutes. Or maybe you had a major customer win that you'd like to walk them through. Or a major shift in strategy. Whatever, You need to push for the next meeting.

Create a Content Generation System

It's important to create a "content generation system" that provides you with daily updates related to your business area. Start by creating a daily Google search on key words related to your field. Augment that with subscriptions to newsletters, conferences, blogs, and so forth. Your objective is to have a repository of current news that you can share with interested parties (like potential investors). Be sure to personalize sharing of these news updates. Try to make a connection between past interactions with the investor and the information you are now sharing. For example, "I thought you might be interested in the attached article. During our recent meeting, you asked about possible uses of our products by primary care physicians. This is an article written by a doctor who is describing such a requirement. I'd be pleased to answer any questions about this type of use. Feel free to call me on my cell phone."

Share Good News

Share good news about your company. It is a good practice to hold back some developing good news from your initial presentation so that you can follow-up in a couple of weeks with positive breaking news. You want to create positive momentum and create an impression that your successes are growing.

The best way to wake up investor interest is to share a significant customer win with them: "[Tech giant] just signed a 90-day evaluation agreement with our firm and will go live with our product next week." On the other hand, be careful about using "futures" to rekindle interest since that can backfire. For example, avoid statements like: "Just got a call from our key contact at [tech giant] and they indicated that might consider demo-ing our product."

Explore Ways to Build Rapport

Always be on the lookout to explore ways to build rapport. During your research about the investor, recall that you should have learned about their other investments and interests. Make note of these items in your spreadsheet and create a Google search for related items. You need to do this sparingly since you do not want to assume a role as a personal secretary, but even a little of this can be a significant differentiator for you and keep your deal on their radar screen.

Many investors have interesting hobbies or other serious interests outside of work. If they look fit, they probably engage in physical activities like cycling, working out, running, golf, tennis, and so forth. Hopefully, during the meeting you were able to learn and mention something about one their favorite non-work activities. If so, you can add that to the items you can work on to establish a closer relationship.

One of my hobbies is playing golf. My office contains some obvious evidence of this through photos, books, a sleeve of balls, and other golf-related items. Every once in a while, an entrepreneur will pick up on this and attempt to broaden their contact with me by sending along golf-related info—or even inviting me to play with them at a desirable location. I am certainly aware of what they are trying to do, but nevertheless, I do react positively to such overtures. Creating added interactions by exploiting common interests is certainly a legitimate part of the fundraising process.

Create Urgency

I saved this for last because this technique must be used carefully or it can easily backfire. There are ways to create urgency that can be effective. First of all, be honest. If your round is filling up and you have limited room and time remaining, feel free to share the news with uncommitted investors. "I just thought I would let you know that we are closing this investment round at the end of the month. Let me know if you are still interested." If you are seeking a lead investor and truly have another offer pending, it is OK to send out an e-mail update: "Just wanted to keep you updated on our fundraising. We really liked your firm and wanted to see if you are still interested. We recently received a term sheet from [another VC firm]." Do not attempt this if you are simply blowing air and do not have a real alternative. Faking it could have career-limiting consequences.

▒ **Note**   If you create urgency designed to get an investor to make a decision, you'd better be sure the reason is legitimate. If you lie about interest from other investors, a technology breakthrough, or customer interest, you will be found out and shunned by the investment community thereafter.

Best Practices for Following Up

Your company's future is on the line and you'd like an investor to commit to funding you. On the one hand, if you're too timid, you won't receive a dime. On the other hand, if you come on too strong, the result will be the same. So you need to walk a fine line that shows you are neither wimpy nor arrogant, but simply confident in your solution. Here are some best practices:

Don't stop communicating until you receive a hard "not interested." You are fully in control of how much effort you put into ongoing communication and you should never give up until you have either raised all the needed funds (in which case you send out an announcement to everyone you met with) or received a hard *no*.

Be persistent, but don't become a pest. Weekly communication is about right. If you have established a dialog on some points, obviously keep your end of it going as frequently as necessary to respond to inquiries. But if all you have is one-sided attempts to get a response, just don't overdo it to the point that you are annoying people.

Keep your communication lighthearted and playful. You don't want to come across as getting mad or hard-boiled due to failed attempts to get responses. Your communication needs to be friendly when you're asking for more meetings. For example: "I'm really sorry to push you, but I guess you'd want to invest in somebody who pushes customers a bit, too, right?" It is easy to cross the line, especially if you are running out of time. Investors smell desperation and lose interest in deals when entrepreneurs signal that they have lost their cool.

Use multiple channels. Many investors' e-mail boxes are overloaded and your e-mails may easily get lost in the clutter. Check in with the office manager (whom, of course, you met in your first meeting and who is now aware of who you are!). Ask him/her for advice on how to best contact the investor. If the investor uses Twitter or Facebook, or prefers texting, try that as well.

Once you get a no, it is time to move on. A hard no means that it is time to thank the investor for giving you an opportunity to interact with them. Ask for referrals to other investors (you never know), and then move on. A soft no can come via extended periods without communication and a lack of success in your requests for feedback. If two to three weeks pass and you have sent four messages that should have been received, you might consider sending an e-mail asking them to verify that they no longer have interest in continuing discussions with you.

Remember that you are building a strategic network. Most investors will continue to be there for future deals, so the rejection of one transaction should not be looked upon as the end but rather the beginning of building long-term relationships that may bear fruit in the future. By all means, invite investors to your LinkedIn database so that you can connect with them over time. Walk up to investors at events that you mutually attend and re-engage them. Let them know of your successes, and continue to build your personal brand and credibility with them. Too often, entrepreneurs give up on investors and fail to think of them as strategic resources that must continue to be cultivated over time.[1]

---

[1] I highly recommend Michael Hyatt's fascinating book, *Platform: Get Noticed in a Noisy World* (Thomas Nelson, 2012). In it, he lays out many great ways to develop and maintain a personal, lifelong PR campaign that will greatly improve your ability to build a personal brand that will not only help you with investors, but in many other important ways as well.

Summary

The following is the most important insight in this book:

Lack of follow-up is the number-one reason deals do not get funded.

These days, nobody can be counted on to write checks at a first meeting. So your follow-up efforts will be critical no matter how well your initial meeting went. Seasoned investors will test your follow-up skills because they know that you will get many "no's" as you grow your business—and they want to know firsthand that you are the type of person that will persevere and overcome objections. I understand that for many entrepreneurs, it is more difficult to pursue and close investors than it is to develop and deliver a great presentation. However, it is critical that you cultivate strong follow-up skills and force yourself to look at your investor follow-up sheet every morning and to set your priorities accordingly.

Even if you only do 50% of what is recommended in this chapter, you will separate yourself from many other entrepreneurs, because most simply drop the ball and fail to capitalize on the initial interest they developed.

Building the Executive Summary

The successful outcome of your initial 12 Magic Slides presentation gives the green light to go forward with the other materials required to close your funding round. Your 12 Magic Slides put you in good shape to complete these remaining materials. And with the tough job of obtaining at least some solid investor interest behind you, you are now ready to shift resources and move on to other necessary items.

To recap, most investors will need to see and review the following:

- A PowerPoint presentation (the 12 Magic Slides)
- Detailed financials (workbook-style, with 3- to 5-year projections, and including a balance sheet, a hiring plan, etc.)
- A capitalization table that summarizes the company ownership positions of all shareholders, and also summarizes various stock classes and option pools
- A technology summary (road map, patent portfolio, "secret sauce")
- Background checks of key executives (performed with your permission)
- Résumés of and references for key personnel

- Customer references
- Bank references
- Videos (optional, but getting more common)
- A subscription agreement and Regulation D SEC filing forms[1]
- A private placement memorandum, including risk disclosures

In addition, investors will require either an executive summary and/or a business plan. If the executive summary is comprehensive and other materials are complete, a business plan may not be required.

The executive summary is simply a narrative that details what you plan to do and how investors will benefit. A standalone executive summary (without a business plan, but with all the other items noted earlier) should be between ten and twenty pages. If a business plan is also available, the executive summary can be as little as two pages and may be the opening section of the full business plan.

In this chapter, I will discuss two important documents from this list: the executive summary and the private placement memorandum.

Note   Covering topics such as Regulation D or Regulation A falls outside the scope of this book. But Googling either of these, or any of the other items in the preceding list, will provide you with plenty of information.

Building the Executive Summary

As you might have gathered by now, I am a big fan of Tom Peter's "ready, fire, aim" approach.[2] It means starting your business creation process using baby steps, getting feedback, tuning, adding a bit more, and so on. I strongly recommend

---

[1] With the passage of the JOBS Act of 2012, use of Regulation A as an alternative to the traditional Regulation D filing process has picked up. Due to certain benefits, including an increased liquidity option, you should evaluate Regulation A as an option.

[2] Tom Peters is a great contemporary writer of books focused on helping entrepreneurs better understand the process of business creation. You owe it to yourself to buy and devour his books and sage advice. Start with *In Search of Excellence* (Harper and Row, 1982), one of his very best works, but also study his other writings on leadership—especially one of my favorites, "Leadership: The 4 Most Important Words," (http://www.tompeters.com/blogs/toms_videos/docs/Leadership_4_Most_Important_Words.pdf).

a process of building various business summaries in which you start with the most basic items and then work your way up to more complex items. In other words, first develop your elevator pitch to land meetings, and then build your first PowerPoint deck, and once you confirm interest from investors, complete the backup documents, executive summary, and so forth.

Along the way, you will also develop your corporate marketing materials, like brochures, videos, a web site, and so forth—all of which is useful in wooing investors.

The executive summary flows right from the first-meeting PowerPoint presentation. As mentioned, it is a narrative that spells out what you plan to do and how investors will benefit. In short, it is the written version of your 12 Magic Slides, with additional details covering the follow-up questions that investors typically ask. In some cases, it substitutes your initial PowerPoint presentation—particularly when it is given to investors and other decision makers who were unable to see you present.

Here's a great way to quickly knock out a good first draft of your executive summary: record one or more of your investor presentations, being sure to include potential questions and comments from your investors. Have the audio file of your recording transcribed into editable text—and, Voila! You will have a first-draft executive summary in no time.[3]

This draft will likely be much longer than what you want to end up with, so you will need to go through several rounds of editing, including making decisions on graphics, testimonials (you always want to include customer quotes and testimonials), and any other special content (e.g., news articles) that you might include. As I mentioned earlier, standalone executive summaries should be in the range of 10 to 20 pages and well organized so that they can be easily reviewed by busy investors. Avoid too much prose and be sure to include graphs, diagrams, and especially key customer quotes. Today's executive summaries often include links to downloadable content, such as videos and larger backup material files (e.g., your full financial workbook).

To offer a Silicon Valley perspective, fundraising here is a lot like dating. You start with getting the investor interested in learning more about you/your business. Then you build a relationship over time that leads to an investment. You don't tell your life story on a first date—and you don't deliver your full business plan in one shot. During the dot-com days, I saw a lot of large checks

---

[3] There are many low-cost, fast turnaround transcription services. Do a web search to find one that meets your needs. One that I like is Rev.com (www.rev.com). There is a lot of turnover in these services, however, and a better one might be on the scene by the time you read this section.

written by investors over a cup of coffee. But after the massive losses that were experienced during the meltdown, investors became much more cautious about reaching for their checkbooks. They want to engage with you over time, share your ideas with their trusted friends for feedback, see how you perform on your commitments to get them more information—and typically only write a check when they are fully convinced that you meet their criteria. The era of blind investing ended with the crash of the stock market in 2001.

Should You Create Both a Business Plan and an Executive Summary?

Business schools suggest that you should always create a business plan. And there are many software companies that advertise templates that make the process of developing a full-blown business plan relatively fast and easy. It is a good discipline to develop a full business plan, since the process mimics the annual planning process that you should conduct with your executive team each year.

Here's the reality: today there is a large availability of various presentation channels, such as PowerPoint slides, web sites, webinars, live video, and so forth, which are more efficient in presenting information than long prose. Also, investors have less of an attention span than they used to and do not want to wade through long documents to determine if your deal is for them.

Finally, for most early-stage businesses, 90% of a business plan is projection and speculation, and it is based more on the desires of the founders to realize attractive objectives. By its very nature, this includes a high degree of risk. Professional investors, such as venture capitalists, are very busy. In my own practice, we receive as many as a dozen solicitations from entrepreneurs a week—and we are a relatively small firm. If we attend group pitch sessions, we could have 20 or more pitches to evaluate on top of our ongoing volume of deals to consider.

The bottom line: VCs don't have the time to sift through business plans; they prefer a more layered approach to their due diligence, starting with a brief introduction and overview, followed by your PowerPoint presentation, and then more if they have interest. If you have prepared all the items listed earlier, and they are current, there is little need to prepare a full business plan in advance. If a business plan becomes a hard requirement because some investor needs to check that box on their due diligence checklist, an acceptable business plan can be quickly assembled from the available materials.

The Private Placement Memorandum

If you are planning to reach out to noninstitutional investors—such as angels, high net worth individuals, investment clubs, and so forth—you will need to prepare a private placement memorandum (PPM), also called an offering memorandum (OM) or an offering circular (OC). It is a formal summary of your business plan, along with comprehensive risk disclosures that are designed to protect you from lawsuits. While the contents of a PPM are very much deal-specific, the following areas are typically included:

- Detailed risk factors

- A legal description of your ownership structure and where you have formally registered

- A summary of your overall business plan, including how you plan to differentiate your firm from your major competitors

- Various disclosures, including possible conflicts of interest or other items that may impact the willingness of investors to invest

- Various backup items, including financial, marketing, sales, or manufacturing data

Among the most important components of the PPM package are the investor questionnaire and the subscription agreement—a legal document that outlines what investors are getting in return for their money, as well as various attestations. These can be two separate documents; however, they are frequently combined in a single standalone document that accompanies the PPM or is often given to the investor prior to obtaining their check. The purpose of these documents is to provide instructions on the mechanics for participating in the offering and to qualify the investor as meeting the requirements for the offering. The questions contained in the investor questionnaire can provide significant liability protection for the company's officers. It needs to be properly developed to cover the range of issues where you may have exposure.

The standards of full disclosure have increased in recent years due to abuses and scandals that have made front-page headlines. In particular, the Securities and Exchange Commission (SEC), which oversees many of the areas related to fundraising, has taken steps to hold entrepreneurs increasingly liable for lack of full disclosure. Investors today also have greater recourse that they can take when deals turn sour, including the ability to hold executives personally responsible for representations that they make. Frankly, we advise all entrepreneurs to develop a PPM using a qualified attorney for each investment round sought. Also use a qualified attorney to create documents that require written affirmation from investors and state that they have read the PPM and understand the nature of the risk factors, as well as other disclosures related to the investment.[4]

The cost of the PPM generally ranges from $5,000 to as much as $30,000 or more, depending on the scope and whom you select to do the related work. In the best case, the PPM will end up in your archive and rarely be referred to, if at all. On the other hand, if the investment falls below expectations or goes sour, the disclosures in the PPM will be your first line of defense against investors seeking damages.

Note　Unfortunately, we live in an increasingly litigious society. There are more and more attorneys who seek out and represent investors in deals gone bad. They chase entrepreneurs on a contingency basis to claim damages and otherwise make your life miserable. While a PPM is not a 100% ironclad guarantee against lawsuits, I strongly recommend that you invest in a proper PPM. Consider the investment in it as the cost of doing business and the closest that you can come to an insurance policy that can provide some protection in a worst-case outcome.

Is There Any Downside to Raising Money with a PPM?

Some sophisticated angel investors will argue that a PPM is a roadblock to obtaining funding. The arguments relate to the fact that the PPM states specific investment terms that are generally not open to further negotiation. Some angels prefer to negotiate investment terms more attractive for them than what entrepreneurs are willing to offer, and they also often regard earlier investors as too friendly with the valuation. Expect to hear the following: "Why should I invest at a high valuation simply because the friends of the founders were too generous?"

Even though some angels will not look at deals that are offered with a PPM, the risks for the entrepreneur are simply too high to avoid the protection that comes with a well-written PPM.

---

[4]The general exceptions to developing a full PPM are with an initial small seed round where the investment sought is too small to justify the costs of a full PPM, or when funds are being raised exclusively from existing investors (a.k.a. "an insider round"). Even in situations where funds are sought from people you may know (friends and family), you should always require that investors complete a comprehensive subscription agreement and investor questionnaire, and sign an acknowledgment of appropriate risk factors. Even if your friends and family trust you and do not even read these documents, it is better to have the signed documents than not.

Should you allow special terms for some investors? Maybe, but it is a slippery slope.

It is not uncommon to negotiate a special one-off deal with a large investor. However, such negotiations and related disclosures need to be handled very carefully, since the existence of special terms that are not offered to all investors can be a basis for legal actions by the other investors coming into that investment round. If you are getting push back on your offering terms from more than a few investors, it is better to revise the PPM with new terms that are offered to all investors and that meet your financial objectives—rather than to do special one-off deals with some investors. If you find yourself in the late stages of closing a round and you are tempted to do a one-off to get the last large tranche in the deal closed, I strongly advise you to obtain advice from an experienced attorney and weigh the risks/rewards very carefully.

Summary

Having covered the importance of various documents, especially the executive summary and the private placement memorandum, it's time to focus on two important outcomes of your presentation. You either got the funding offer that you've been looking for—congratulations!—or you were turned down. The next chapter explores both outcomes.

You Got a Deal! Or Not...

Congratulations on completing the prior chapters! I hope your investment of time in learning how to present the 12 Magic Slides will prove to be very profitable now and in the future. (Remember, this format works at any fundraising step, from start-up to IPO.)

Many of the entrepreneurs who completed our past workshops have indicated that exposure to the 12 Magic Slides process made a permanent impact on how they tackle their fundraising efforts, and also in the way they look at and question future deals that they may personally consider investing in. Hopefully, you have now developed a more critical eye for looking at new deals—and will also apply more rigorous standards to your own fundraising efforts.

First, What If You Strike Out?

While the approach to fundraising outlined in this book is time-tested and has resulted in many successful fundraising campaigns, it will not overcome fundamental problems in a flawed business plan. In fact, using the 12 Magic Slides process often exposes shortcomings much earlier in the fundraising process and allows you the time to either address and correct issues or, in a worst case, cause you to abandon the pursuit of your business idea. (And yes, sometimes this is the best course, because it frees you sooner to find a better opportunity.)

In fact, many of the entrepreneurs who learned the 12 Magic Slides approach failed to obtain funding due to issues with their business plan, but not as a result of how it was presented. Within a relatively short amount of time, however, I often saw these same entrepreneurs developing a new and better opportunity. And by following the 12 Magic Slides principles, they were able to achieve a successful outcome the next time around. Most said that what they learned through using the 12 Magic Slides approach helped them target more attractive and fundable business opportunities, which resulted in a better use of their talents and resources.

Note   Sometimes not getting funded is the best outcome. It helps you refine or redefine the opportunity and increases your chances of getting funded the next time around.

As all experienced entrepreneurs will attest, the path to a successful fund-raising effort is full of rejection. It will come in many forms, starting with the frequent "I am not interested" response to first meetings that do not go further. Rejection also comes in the form of false positives (like "maybe") that often lead to dead ends. If you face up to this, it will be easier to overcome the challenges. In my experience, the most successful entrepreneurs maintain confidence in themselves and continue to inspire their team members to keep moving forward. They treat negative responses as opportunities to learn something useful in making their next pitch more effective.

Most professional investors will be honest with you, and if asked, will tell you why they are not investing in your deal. Often, there will not be much you can do ("We are not investing in deals in your space at this time"). But there will also be opportunities to learn something that will lead to success with subsequent investors or perhaps allow you to reapproach investors who initially turned you down.

While there is no substitute for hard work and tenacious follow-up, things that you can't always count on, like luck and timing, also play a huge role. Many good ideas with great teams fail simply because they are ahead of their time. For example, during the dot-com era, there were many new and creative ideas that required faster Internet performance and access to mobile devices that were not available at that time. Similarly, many former big ideas had their day, made their founders and investors rich, and then disappeared.[1]

---

[1]As I'm writing this, Blockbuster announced it was closing its last store. At the same time, Netflix's profits are near all-time highs. Go figure!

Increase Your Chances of Funding the Next Time

Although you can't have much control over luck and timing, there are a number of factors that I have observed that can increase both your chances of raising funds and/or being part of winning team.

- Invest in your personal education to the greatest extent possible. Stick to solid courses that can make you more successful in the business world, like math, science, engineering, accounting, business, and law. Push yourself to take tougher classes and to try to get into the best schools that you can afford.

- Seek opportunities to build personal discipline and leadership capabilities. Joining sports teams, civic or social organizations, or having a stint in the military can help develop such skills at an accelerated rate.

- Aggressively seek and try to make lifelong friends with outstanding individuals, including classmates, business associates, and people that you meet while networking. The vast majority of successful founding teams are composed of people that previously knew each other. It is human nature to want to work with folks whom you like and admire—and there are many very successful entrepreneurs whose close friend got the idea that made both of them rich.

- A good track record trumps a lot of other shortcomings. If you are short in this department, focus on aligning yourself with people who have a stronger track record than you do; ideally, those who have at least one notable business success and who are recognized by your potential investors. If this means playing second fiddle, don't let pride get in the way of your success. Be content to be on a winning team, even if you are not the leader. Many leaders did not start at the top—but eventually got there. (Marissa Mayer, current CEO of Yahoo!, started out as employee 20 at Google.) Also, if you are building your track record, seek employment opportunities in successful firms. If your current firm is not a rising star, polish your résumé and join a firm that is—even if you need to take a lower-grade starting position.

- As the saying goes, you need to be in the middle of the road to get hit by a car. Presume that success will rarely come knocking on your door. You need to get out of your comfort zone and meet a lot of people. See others in action so that you can increase your odds of coming across a life-altering opportunity. If you are really committed to building your career and personal success, you need to make networking and relationship-building a top priority. Use of social media like LinkedIn, Facebook, and Twitter is increasingly important. However, there is nothing better than meeting and interacting with people who can have a positive impact on your career face to face. Seek out and participate in appropriate meet-and-greet venues. Plan to attend, or better yet, find opportunities to speak on panels at industry conferences. Invest in building closer relationships with the superstars that you meet.

- At all times, be honest with yourself and those around you. Once you let down your guard in this area, you are on a slippery slope and can short circuit your career. Sure, there are examples of ruthless executives who get rich—but those role models will not serve you well.

As you lay out your game plan for using the 12 Magic Slides on your next fundraising campaign, also review and act on these suggestions to increase your odds of success. By the way, you are never too young or too old to get started. Recall my example of Mark Zuckerberg's early successes, which fit many of these observations. And if you think that you are too old to get retooled, think again. Earlier this year we successfully raised a mezzanine capital round for a medical diagnostic company. We are currently assisting them to go public on the NASDAQ stock exchange. The founder/chairman is 85 years old!

If you keep at the process of looking for new opportunities to solve big customer problems, and increase your odds of success through following the suggestions in this chapter, you will greatly increase the likelihood of realizing your ambitions, even if your first attempts fall short.

After a Successful First Meeting

Let's say that your first efforts with using the 12 Magic Slides succeeded in getting you additional meetings with an investor. Well done! So what's next?

Beginning shortly after a successful first meeting, you will begin to discuss investment terms with your target investors. All funding rounds are subject to terms and conditions detailed in a document called a "term sheet." The term sheet not only sets the price of the ownership interests that will be acquired, but also spells out many more details related to protecting the interests of current owners/investors (you) and the new outside investors. In some cases, such as when your opportunity is attracting more investors than needed, the company and its current investors can dictate the terms of the new investment on a "take it or leave it" basis. In other cases, a lead outside investor may emerge, who will significantly influence the terms of the offering. The scope of topics to be considered and negotiated is highly situation-dependent and can be quite complex, often requiring the services of a knowledgeable securities attorney.

I highly recommend that you locate and study term sheets that show how investments are structured for comparable firms in your industry. These documents should be available from attorneys, accountants, and investment bankers. I also recommend an excellent book that you should read to become familiar with all the related terms and concepts—*Venture Deals: Be Smarter Than Your Lawyer and Venture Capitalist* (Wiley, 2011) by Brad Feld and Jason Mendelson.

As your term sheet is being finalized, and you are completing follow-up meetings, you will also be completing other related materials, including a subscription agreement, an investor questionnaire, and various disclosure materials (like the private placement memorandum discussed in the last chapter). Although you can find many templates for these types of documents on the Internet, I strongly advise you to hire a competent attorney and not attempt a do-it-yourself effort that will reflect poorly on you with your investors. If you are short on funds, find an attorney who may consider lowering his or her fees by taking some compensation in the form of stock options.

Tip Remember, your fundraising efforts are not over until all the paperwork is executed and the money is in your bank account. As soon as you have developed adequate investor interest to fund your investment round, develop a checklist of all the items necessary to fully close the investment; do this with input from your attorney. Schedule frequent follow-up meetings with your attorney to ensure that everything is completed on time.

The Road Ahead

More than 30 years ago, when I first came to Silicon Valley and joined my first start-up, I attended local networking meetings where local luminaries told young entrepreneurs like me that there was no better time than the present to start a new businesses. That observation remains true to this day, and with all the added resources that entrepreneurs have at their disposal, the odds of being successful in starting and growing new businesses continue to improve. Unlike the environment that I faced when taking my first steps as an entrepreneur, there are now many proven best practices that can be learned and utilized to dramatically improve your ability to realize your ambitions.

I thank all of you who have taken the time to learn the 12 Magic Slides. I hope that the materials and insights that I have shared make a very positive impact on your future endeavors. Good luck!

Index

Get the eBook for only $10!

Now you can take the weightless companion with you anywhere, anytime. Your purchase of this book entitles you to 3 electronic versions for only $10.

This Apress title will prove so indispensible that you'll want to carry it with you everywhere, which is why we are offering the eBook in 3 formats for only $10 if you have already purchased the print book.

Convenient and fully searchable, the PDF version enables you to easily find and copy code—or perform examples by quickly toggling between instructions and applications. The MOBI format is ideal for your Kindle, while the ePUB can be utilized on a variety of mobile devices.

Go to www.apress.com/promo/tendollars to purchase your companion eBook.

Apress®
THE EXPERT'S VOICE™

Other Apress Business Titles You Will Find Useful

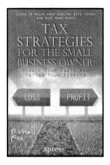

Tax Strategies for the Small Business Owner
Fox
978-1-4302-4842-2

Plan Your Own Estate
Wheatley-Liss
978-1-4302-4494-3

Getting a Business Loan
Kiisel
978-1-4302-4998-6

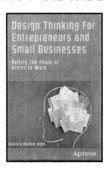

Design Thinking for Entrepreneurs and Small Businesses
Ingle
978-1-4302-6181-0

Improving Profit
Cleland
978-1-4302-6307-4

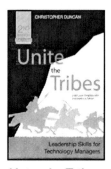

Unite the Tribes, 2nd Edition
Duncan
978-1-4302-5872-8

Healthcare, Insurance, and You
Zamosky
978-1-4302-4953-5

Common Sense
Tanner
978-1-4302-4152-2

When to Hire—or Not Hire—a Consultant
Orr/Orr
978-1-4302-4734-0

Available at www.apress.com

CPSIA information can be obtained
at www.ICGtesting.com
Printed in the USA
LVOW11s1435130817

544850LV00003B/318/P